LEARN PYTHON PROGRAMMING FOR BEGINNERS

Lewis Smith

Ready to learn programming now
this is your time!

by the trademark owner. All trademarks and brands within this book are for clarifying purposes only and are owned by the owners themselves, not affiliated with this document.

TABLE OF CONTENES

5

INTRODUZION

Whether your goal is to launch a career in the lucrative world of software development or to simply make some money on the side while you are still in college, Python is your ideal choice. Here's why Python can run on all popular operating systems, including Linux, Windows, and Mac OS. For the Mac OS version, you will need to install the XCode developer tools. The latest version is recommended. Python's simplicity and adaptability make the language ideal for scripting.

Many software programs in the WordPress and web development industries are written in Python. This means there is an abundance of free resources that are available and waiting to be tapped by the aspiring developer. In addition, Python's Web Development Tools page is a valuable resource for learning Python. It has links to resources, such as code editors, deployment servers, and e-books. This page also gives an explanation of the capabilities and compatibility of Python.

For the beginning coder, Python is one of the easiest languages to learn and use. You do not need to learn other languages, such as C++, to use the language. On the same note, Python's simple syntax allows new programmers to understand and use the language quickly. The creators of Python aimed to make a language that would be easy for programmers to learn while also giving the creator enough flexibility to write practically invisible code. Python is also relatively easy to use since there are pre-built libraries, such as PRAW.

Here is another great resource -- a free course on Coursera that will teach you Python in just twelve insightful lectures. You don't have to be a big-name developer to get started with Python. There are many schools across the world that teach Python using online courses. You will learn to take an idea, code it up on the web, and get it online. In the industry, this can mean making a website, a mobile app, or even a video game. In fact, you can get started building web applications with Python as fast as you can code. Using Python, you can reuse code made by other developers because Python is a highly versatile language. You can build websites with advanced functionality that can have users input data and pick orders.

The tutorials range from simple "Hello World" applications to real-world design elements. It doesn't matter how much you already know about Python because Programming for Beginners is the perfect Python learning resource for everyone. Instead of finding your code on the Internet, you can find the code that you need from scratch and make it work. Here is another fantastic Python resource -- Python Tutor, an awesome Python tutorial site for learning the language. This is a comprehensive course that will teach you both the high-level and advanced features of

Python. The Python Tutor is an excellent place to learn the C programming language for Python. It covers a wide variety of topics, ranging from web services to the Python Difflib library. The Python Tutor also teaches you the Python programming basics and provides a high-level introduction to Python.

WHAT IS PYTHON?

This is a programming language that is object-oriented and of high level and uses semantics. It is a high level in terms of structures in data and a combination of dynamic typing and binding. This is what makes it attractive to be used for Rapid Application Development and for connecting different elements.

Python, with its simplicity and learning with ease, helps in reading the programming language, and that is why it reduces the cost to maintain the program. Python encourages program modularity and code reuse; this is because it supports different packages and modules. The standard library and the Python interpreter can be found in binary form. It is not necessary to charge all the available platforms and can be distributed freely.

Most programmers love the Python program because they offer great productivity. The edit-test debug is a cycle that is fast and does not need any compilation process. It is easier to debug a Python program; it will not cause any segmentation fault. An exception is raised when an error is discovered by the interpreter. When the exception is not known by the program, the interpreter prints a trace. The debugger, on a level of sourcing, will allow being inspecting any variables. There will be a settling of breakpoints, arbitrary expressions, and stepping on the code at any time. The Python is what writes the debugger, the easier, and a quick debugging method and programs of adding prints on the source and statements.

Python is open-source; this means you can use them freely for any commercial applications. Python is programmed to work on UNIX, Windows, and Mac and can be transferred to Java. Python is a language that helps in scripting and helps in web applications for different content.

It is like Perl and Ruby. Python is helped by several imaging programs; users are able to create customized extensions. There are different web applications supporting Python API like Blender and GIMP.

This information given on Python programming is beneficial for both the newbies and the experienced ones. Most of the experienced programmers can easily learn and use Python. There is an easier way to install Python. Most distributors of UNIX and Linux have the recent Python. That is the reason why most computers are already installed with Python. Before you start using Python, you need to know which IDEs and text editors' best work with Python. To get more help and information, you can peruse introductory books and code samples.

The Python idea was discovered in 1980 after the ABC language. Python 2.0 was introduced; it had features like garbage collection and list comprehensions, which are used in reference cycle collection. When Python 3.0 was released in 2008, it brought about a complete language revision. Python is primarily used for developing software and webs, for mathematics and scripting systems. The latest version of Python is known a Python 3 while Python 2 is still popular. Python was developed to help in reading and similar aspects to different languages like English and emphasis on Mathematics. A new line is used to complete a Python command, as opposed to other programming languages that normally use semi-colons. It depends on indentation, whitespace, and defining the scope.

How to Use Python Programming?

Before using Python, you first need to install and run it on your computer, and once you do that, you will be able to write your first program. Python is known as a programming platform that cuts across multiple platforms. You can use it on Linux, macOS, Windows, Java, and .NET machines freely and as an open-source. Most of the Linux and Mac machines come preinstalled even though on an outdated version. That is the main reason why you will need to install the latest and current version. An easier way to run Python is by using Thonny IDE; this is bundled with the latest Python version. This is an advantage since you will not need to install it separately.

To achieve all that, you can follow the simple steps below:

1. First, you will need to download Thonny's IDE.
2. Then run the installer to install it on your computer.

Click on the File option, then new. Save the file on the .py extension, for instance, morning.py or file.py. You are allowed to use any name for the file, as long as it ends with .py. Write the Python code on the file before saving it.

3. To run the file, click on RUN, the run current script. Alternatively, click on F5 to run it.

There is also an alternative to install Python separately; it does not involve installing and running Python on the computer. You will need to follow the listed steps below:

1. Look for the latest version of Python and download it.
2. The next step is to run the installer file to install Python.
3. When installing, look for Add Python to environment variables. This will ensure that Python is added to the environment variables, enabling you to run Python from any computer destination and part. You have the advantage of choosing the path to install Python.
4. When you complete the process of installing, you can now run Python.

There is also an alternative and immediate mode to run Python. When Python is installed, you will type Python on the command line; the interpreter will be in immediate mode. You can type Python code, and when you press enter, you will get the output. For instance, when you type 1 + 1 and then press enter, you will get the output as 2. You can use it as a calculator, and you quit the process, type quit, then press enter.

The second way to do it is by running Python on the Integrated Development Environment. You can use any editing software to write the Python script file. All you need to do is save the extension .py, and it is considered a lot easier when you use an IDE. The IDE is a feature that has distinctive and useful features like file explorers, code hinting, and syntax checking and highlighting that a programmer can use for application development.

You need to remember that when you install Python, there is an IDE labeled IDLE that will also be installed.

That is what you will use to run Python on the computer, and it is considered the best IDE for beginners. You will have an interactive Shell when IDLE is opened. This is where you can have a new file and ensure that you save it as a .py extension.

PROGRAMMING LANGUAGE EXPLANATION

Learning a programming language enables a person to begin coding. So, which programming language should a beginner start learning? The programming languages offer varying features, which means no straight and correct answer to this question.

Instead, an individual should evaluate his or her needs to determine which programming language they should start learning. He or she should also consider aspects such as dedicated community and intuitive syntax to aid in choosing where to begin. There is a saying, "Start as you mean to go on," and it applies here. A person who identifies and learns the right language will eventually be ready to learn to program effectively and successfully.

Easiest Programming Languages for Beginners

Below are some of the simplest programming languages that first-time learners can study and put in use. Understanding how they function will help a person to determine which programming language to start learning.

1. Python

Python is a programming language that a person utilizes to form desktop and web applications. He or she uses it as a vital tool in scientific computing, machine learning, and data mining. Python provides one of the easiest and best programming languages for those at a beginner level. It also enables users to convey the idea of interest fully while using fewer lines of code.

Guido van Rossum created this programming language in the 1980s as a free and open-source language kind. Python is easy to employ because it is flexible, procedural, contains dynamic language, and is oriented to object (OOP). Additionally, it also offers functional programming styles. Many people mention Python very quickly in any talks concerning coding due to its popularity among teachers and learners. Many schools in Europe and the United States commonly provide Python in the introduction phase during the courses involving programming languages.

Python is an ideal programming language for a beginner to learn because it is straightforward and offers some fun when writing. Beginners find the Python program's syntax to be less strange, not intimidating, and more comfortable to process. The Python source code used in this programming utilizes only white space, making the source code appear similar from one project to

17

another. Furthermore, Python provides the Pythonic approach to coding, which is essentially the right way to encrypt. Thus, correctly writing the Pythonic code allows the beginner learner to read and comprehend it easily.

Additionally, a person can find tutorials regarding the Python programming language easily due to its popularity among users. Research and knowledge are fundamental to any learning process. Hence, readily accessible Python tutorials are a huge benefit for beginners. Some tutorials help a person to have a sense and familiarity with the language. Likewise, some sites or courses provide more interactive methods to comprehend the programming language further.

Learning the Python programming language is useful because many applications and fields apply it in their development. It uses web frameworks like Django to enable developers to create and power different back-end features and applications. It also provides dictionaries and libraries such as SciPy, which a person uses to initiate a particular project. As a result, Python enables development to proceed rapidly.

Therefore, Python is an excellent programming language for a beginner to learn. It is free, easy to understand, and offers some benefit to its future application.

2. JavaScript

JavaScript is a programming language that an individual uses to develop web, mobile, and web apps. Most modern browsers run this programming language. It provides a cross-platform nature that makes it easy for a beginner to learn which, in turn, makes it a popular programming language. All web browsers support JavaScript and can provide scripting, along with server-side languages, such as when using Node.js.

A person mainly uses JavaScript in front-end development that offers scripting language on the client-side. It provides an excellent introductory programming language for beginners despite receiving fewer recommendations than Python and Ruby programming languages. This shortcoming is because JavaScript is a programming language that does not use typing. Consequently, a person discovers any errors associated with the runtime.

It is also important to note that beginners should not confuse JavaScript with Java. Java is a programming language, while JavaScript is primarily a scripting language for front-end development. JavaScript is vital in web development and learning; it allows the person to understand the programming language basics. In addition, it also prepares him or her for further education related to web development, as well as C programming language. It is because the syntax of the C programming is similar to that of the JavaScript programming language.

It provides a solid education for beginners because it has a range of applicability. JavaScript programming language involves dynamical-typing or untyped, and it is also more relenting compared to other kinds. It is cross-platform, enabling a person to function without a compiler as it runs in his or her browser. This feature makes it a popular programming language among users and learners. A beginner can also learn using JavaScript to access other complex programming languages such as C++.

A beginner may face some setbacks linked with JavaScript such as issues concerning untyped features where they do not show errors until runtime. However, a beginner can carry out some appropriate research that will enable him or her to comprehend JavaScript easily. It offers various benefits like cross-platform compatibility, among others. These advantages make it valid as an introductory programming language as it is the language of the web.

3. Ruby

Ruby is a programming language that facilitates multiple paradigms such as imperative, functional, and object-oriented programming. As a result, Ruby is a very adaptable programming language that assists a learning beginner in several ways. A person employs the Ruby programming language when developing applications based on the web, mobile apps, and websites.

Ruby provides a syntax that people can read easily. It contains a general-purpose and dynamic language that a beginner not only finds readable but straightforward as well. This syntax enables a person to learn many things, and use the programming without necessarily studying other numerous jargon and commands. An individual employs the Ruby programming language when dealing with the back-end development of his or her work.

Ruby on Rails refers to a web framework based on the Ruby programming language. It comprises a group of Ruby shortcuts. A beginner can learn Ruby on Rails and use it to develop web applications, such as a web blog in a matter of minutes. Learning Ruby and its associated framework like Ruby on Rails can help a person in several ways. It can enable him or her to gain knowledge and skills in a commonly used programming language. It also helps them get jobs because even the beginner level of expertise is highly valuable to various startups.

4. Java

Java is one of the most dependable and influential programming languages around. A person uses Java programming language to develop native applications on Android. He or she can also employ it as a server-side language. James Gosling developed it in the 1990s, and Oracle currently maintains it. Thus, Oracle's Java is among the oldest programming languages that exist.

Java is a programming language that is class-based and object-oriented. Therefore, it allows for the application of cross-platform and portability. Java usually is available during later or advanced stages in school because it utilizes syntax derived from other programming languages like C and C++. Nevertheless, it is also helpful to a beginner because it enables them to develop a thinking process similar to a programmer.

Even though Java builds many of its syntaxes on C or C++, it is still necessary for a beginner to know it. He or she learns and comprehends information processing on a PC. In turn, this knowledge provides a strong foundation for further coding learning and career. The analytical programming knowledge that a beginner gains from learning Java helps them use it and address any problems connected to Java. Moreover, many questions or challenges relating to Java already have answers or solutions since it is one of the oldest programming languages.

Hence, the beginners learning Java may need to start by learning about C or C++ and developing their analytical thinking skills. Despite this setback, Java offers many benefits to the learner because it is a standard programming language with many resources. It provides a long-standing language and a solid programming foundation. The beginner can start and grow his or her programming skills. He or she can then effectively utilize Java in the subsequent application and web development.

5. PHP

PHP is a programming language that an individual utilizes to maintain scripts and develop websites. It is the most common server-side programming language, and it provides server-side scripting. Additionally, it can also create graphics and templates, create desktop operations and command-line scripts. PHP programming language offers a code that makes it easy for a learner to envision how it functions.

As a result, PHP is ideal for a beginner because they can perceive the code functionality use the programming language's versatility. PHP can apply to any significant operating system and enable the use of procedural or/and object-oriented programming. It helps a beginner to learn and understand the simple aspects of the programming language. It also helps him or her access wide-ranging programming aspects, which they can apply in other complicated processes.

6. C and C++

C and C++ programming languages developed many parts of game engines, mobile apps, games, desktop apps, software, and operating systems. The C programming language helps to define the basics because it is among the essential programming languages in the field of computer science. Hence, a beginner will likely learn the C and C++ programming languages before moving on to others.

C programming language utilizes complicated code in comparison to others but still makes the basics clear. For this reason, a beginner needs to learn it despite the complexity of coding that it provides. C++ bases upon the C programming language and is one of the most critical programming languages around. It includes enhancement whereby; it enables object-oriented programming. It also allows a person to understand how things and information work in computer science.

A beginner mainly concerned with game development can start by learning the C++ programming language because it features a lot in developing games and game engines. C++ may be slightly more challenging to learn than C, but it offers many rewards to those who successfully overcome it. Thus, a beginner learning C and C++ programming languages gain valuable background knowledge of computer science. He or she also learns how to apply C and C++ in software and game development.

7. **C#**

C# is a programming language developed by Microsoft that a person uses in web and application development. It is excellent for beginners because it provides an Integrated Drive Electronics (IDE) that is simple to use and wide-ranging. The syntax in C# bases upon the C programming language. Hence, it helps the learner gain a solid foundation in computer science since C provides the field's primary programming languages.

C# contains multiple and complex compilers and interpreters which may be a setback for first-time learners. However, the easy to utilize IDE, computer science background, and Visual Studio make C# ideal for a beginner to learn and use. Visual Studio simplifies the startup process and offers features like auto-generated files and auto-complete.

CREATION AND CUSTOMIZATION OF WEB APPS

A web application runs on a remote server as a software application. Most of the time, web browsers are for web applications like the internet. Some of the applications are used for intranets, schools, firms, and organizations. They are not the same as other applications, since you do not need to install them. Some of the common web applications include Flickr, Wikipedia, Facebook, and Mibbit. They are popular as most operating systems are on the web browser and programmers can change them with ease.

Several benefits come with using web application:

• They do not need to be installed since they run inside a browser.

• They do not require a lot of space for storage; only a display of data is needed.

• Web applications help with compatibility problems; all that is needed is a browser.

• Most of the data used is remotely stored; hence, ease of cooperation and communication.

• Web application helps in mail and communication.

Apart from the listed benefits of web applications, there are also drawbacks:

• Most of the known web applications seem to look different as compared to the regular programs. The reason is that they run inside a browser. The user experience might be different and not liked by many.

• To follow standards, web applications need to be coded, and any small changes will prevent the web application from being used in any browser.

• There is a need to have a connection between the web application and the server in order for it to run smoothly. For the connection to happen, you will need bandwidth. When the connection is not adequate, you may experience data loss or the application may be unstable.

• Most of the web applications depend on the server that hosts them. The web application is not usable when it is off, but the traditional applications will still work.

• The overall control of the web application is with the mother company. They have the power to create a new version when they feel like it.

• When the data is remotely stored, exporting it to be used by other applications will be hard.

• Web applications enable the company to track all the activities of the users, hence privacy issues.

At this point, you need to know how a web application works. Most of the web applications are coded in a language that is browser supported, like HTML or JavaScript. The main reason is that the languages depend on the browser to execute their programs. Others are considered static, and will not need any processing from the server.

When you have a web application, you will need a webserver to manage all the client's requests. The server will help in performing all the tasks, and store data and information. The application servers include ASP, PHP, and JSP. A normal web application has a specific flow:

• The user will trigger a request using the internet that goes to the webserver. This can be done through the web browser or user interface on the application.

• The web server will then forward that request to the specific web application server.

• The requested task will be performed by the web application server; this includes querying the database and data processing that will generate the required results.

• The results will be sent to the web server by the web application server; this is concerning the data processed or the required information.

• The client will get a response from the web server; they will get the information they have requested on the user's display.

How to Work with Django

Django is used to create web applications. It is specifically meant to create a web application that connects to a database. You can also deal with user management, good security, and internationalization. Some of the common web applications include Disqus, Pinterest, and Instagram. You can use Django as standalone libraries, even though it will require extra work. That is the reason why it is not advisable to use it as a standalone tool.

Django is a combination of different components that work by responding to user requests.

The first step is having the request-or-response system. The main work is to receive and return web responses. Django will accept all the URLs' requests and return all the HTML information to the web browser. The page can be in plain text or something better.

The web requests will enter the Django application through the URLs. The only entry point for any Django application is the URL; developers control available URLs. When you access the URL, Django will enable the viewing.

The views will process all your requests. Django views are considered to be codes generated from Python, when the URL is accessed. Views are something simple like returning a text to the user. The text can be made complex. It can be form processing, credit card processing, and database querying. When the view has completed processing, a web response is sent to the user.

When a web response is returned, the user can access the URL on the browser to access the response. This could be an HTML web page that shows a combination of images and text. They are created using the template system from Django.

With Django information, there is the flexibility to have more applications. You can use that you create a simple blog, mobile applications, or desktop. Sites like Instagram and Pinterest power the Django framework.

User Accounts

A user account is on the network server used to store the username of the computer, password, and any relevant information. When you have the user account, it will allow you or not to connect with other computers or networks. With a network with multiple users, you will need user accounts. A good example of a user account is your email account.

There are different types of user accounts, regardless of the operating system that you are using. You will be able to trace, authenticate, and monitor all the services. When you install an operating system, it creates user accounts to have access after the installation. After the installation, you will have four user accounts: system account, super user account, regular and guest user account.

• System account: These are accounts that are used to access resources in the system. The operating system will use these accounts to know if a service is allowed to access the resources or not. When they are installed, they create relevant accounts. After installation, the account will be able to access the needed information. If you are a network or system administrator, you will not need to know the accounts.

• Super user account: This account is privileged in the operating system. When one is using Windows, the account is referred to as the Administrator account. When using Linux, the account is the root account, and the operating system will help the user with completely different tasks. Tasks are like starting services, creating and deleting new user accounts, installing new software, and changing system files.

• Regular user account: This account does not have many privileges and cannot make changes in the system properties and files. They only operate on tasks they are authorized to, like running applications, creating files, and customizing variables.

• The Guest user account: This is the account with less privilege; you will not be able to change anything with the system. The account performs temporary tasks like playing games, watching movies, or browsing the internet. Using Windows, this account will be created after installation; in Linux, you will need to create the account manually after installation.

The next step is to know how to create a user account. When you have multiple users using the same computer, you will need to have new user accounts for each user. When using Windows, you can create several accounts. Each of the user accounts has its settings. It will allow you to control the files separately, and when each user logs in, it will be like their own computer.

The first step in creating a user account is to click on Start on the Control Panel then click on Add or Remove User Accounts. Click on Create a New Account and choose the account type. You will enter the account name, and then select the account type that you wish to create. The administrator has the privilege to create and change accounts, and install programs. The difference is a standard user cannot perform such tasks. The last step will be to click on the Create Account button and close the Control Panel.

How to Style and Deploy an App

Different deployment options need to be considered. When an app is developed in the application builder, it is created in the workplace. All the workplaces have IDs and names; all you need is to create an application in the development, and then deploy it in production.

During deployment, you will decide where you want the existing ID in the workplace; in the existing HTTP server, or a new one. The deployment options are given below.

You will first create an application that is expressed by end-users. The best way to deploy an application is by creating an Application Express for end users. Then, send the URL and login details to the users. It will work when the user population is tolerant and small.

You will need to use the same schema and workplace. You need to export and then import the application, then install it under a different application ID. This strategy will work when there are fewer changes to any known objects.

Use the same schema and a different workplace; export all, and then import the applications into another workplace. It will prevent any production and modification by developers.

Use a different schema and workspace. Export and then import the application into a separate workplace, and install it in a separate schema.

Use a different database for all variations. Export, then import to another Oracle application, and then install it to a different database and schema.

To deploy an app, in the configuration manager console, click on Software Library. Go to Application Management, and then choose Application or Application Group.

Choose from an application or application group in the deploy list, and click Deploy.

OPERATORS IN PYTHON

Why Are Operators Necessary?

One of the main characteristics of a computer is that it has strong computing power. It inputs the data obtained from the outside into the computer, carries out operations through programs, and finally outputs the desired results. In this chapter, we will discuss various types and functions of operators in Python and how to use Python to design expressions for arithmetic calculation and logical judgment.

No matter how complex the program is, the ultimate goal is to help us complete all kinds of operations, and the process must rely on one expression to complete. The expression is just like the usual mathematical formula,

For example: first=(second+third)*(first+10)/3.

The above mathematical formula is an expression; the =,+,* and/sign are operators, and variables first, second, three, and constants 10 and 3 are operands. An expression consists of an operator and an operand.

What Are Operands and Operators?

From the following simple expression (which is also a program statement): first = second+5 the above expression contains three operands first, second, and 5, an assignment operator "=," and an addition operator "+." In addition to arithmetic operators, Python also has comparison operators and logical operators applied to conditional judgment expressions.

In addition, there is an assignment operator that assigns the result of the operation to a variable. Operator if there is only one operand, it is called "unary operator," such as "-23" which expresses negative value. When there are two operands, they are called "binocular operators." Arithmetic operators such as addition, subtraction, multiplication, and division are called "binocular operators," such as 3+7. These various and fully functional operators have different operation priorities. This chapter will introduce the usage of these operators in detail.

Arithmetic operator

This is the most frequently used operator in programming languages. It is commonly used for some four operations, such as addition operator, subtraction operator, multiplication operator, division operator, remainder operator, division operator, exponent operator, etc. The +, -, *, and/operators are the same as our common mathematical operation methods, while the sign operator is mainly used to represent the positive/negative value of operands.

Usually, the + sign can be omitted when the constant is set to a positive number.

For example, "first=5" and "first=+5" have the same meaning. In particular, we should remind everyone that negative numbers are also represented by the "-" operator. When negative numbers participate in subtraction, in order to avoid confusion with subtraction operators, it is better to separate negative numbers with small brackets "()."

"/"and "//"are both division operators. The operation result of "/"is a floating-point number. The "//"will remove the decimal part of the division calculation result and only takes the integer. The "%" operator is the remainder.

For example:

first= 5

second= 2

Print(first/second) # result is floating-point number 2.5

Print(first// second) # result is integer 2

Print(first% second) # Result Is Remainder 1

If the result of the operation is not assigned to other variables, the data type of the operation result will be dominated by the variable whose data type occupies the largest memory space in the operand. In addition, when the operands are integers, and the operation result will produce decimals, Python will automatically output the result as decimals. We do not need to worry about the conversion of data types.

However, if the operation result is to be assigned to a variable, the memory space occupied by the variable must be large enough to prevent the excessively long part of the operation result data from being discarded. For example, if the result of the operation is a floating-point number and is assigned to an integer variable, the decimal part of the operation result will be truncated.

The division "/"operator in the arithmetic operator is a conventional division. The quotient obtained after the operation is a floating-point number. If the quotient is expressed as an integer, the int () function can be called.

Int(15/7) # Output 2 "* *" is a power operation, for example, to calculate the fourth power of 2:

print(7** 4) # The result is 28

Note that the priority of arithmetic operators +, -, *, and/is "multiply and divide first, then add and subtract." The following example illustrates that the operation result of the above formula of 10+2*3 is 16. In the expression, the precedence of parentheses is higher than in multiplication and division.

If the above expression is changed to (10+2)*3, the operation result will be 36. If operators with the same priority are encountered, the operations are performed from left to right. Let's take a look at the application of the simple four operations with an example program.

This sample program allows users to input Celsius temperature and convert it to Fahrenheit temperature through program operation.

The formula for converting Celsius temperature to Fahrenheit temperature is F=(9/5)*C+32.

[sample procedure: sampletemp.py]

Celsius temperature is converted to Fahrenheit temperature

-*- coding: utf-8 -*-

#converts the input Celsius temperature into Fahrenheit temperature

Tip: F = (9/5) * C+32

Celsius = float(input ("Give the Celsius temperature"))

Fahren = (9 / 5) * Celsius + 32

The execution results of the 08 print ("Celsius temperature {0} is converted to Fahrenheit temperature {1}."format(C,F)).

Program Code Resolution:
Line 02: Let the user input Celsius temperature and call float () function to convert the input into a floating-point data type.

Line 03: Converts the input Celsius temperature to Fahrenheit.

Line 04: Output the conversion between Celsius and Fahrenheit according to the specified format string. Incidentally, the "+" sign can be used to connect two strings.

sample="mno"+"pqrs"

result sample = "mnopqrs"

Assignment operator

The assignment operator "=" consists of at least two operands. Its function is to assign the value to the right of "=" to the variable to the left of the equal sign. Most beginners of many programming languages cannot understand the meaning of the equal sign "=" in programming languages.

It is easy to confuse it with the mathematical equivalent function. In programming languages, the "=" sign is mainly used for assignment, but we understand it from a mathematical point of view, and "=" used to be considered as the concept of "equal."

For example, the following program statement:

addition = 0;

addition= addition + 1;

The meaning of addition=0 in the above program statement is also easy to understand, but for the statement addition=addition+1, many beginners often cannot understand the meaning of this statement. In fact, the "=" in Python programming language is mainly used for "assignment."

We can imagine that when a variable is declared, the memory will be allocated, and the memory address will be arranged. Only when the specific value is set to the variable by using the assignment operator "=" will the memory space corresponding to the memory address be allowed to store the specific value.

In other words, addition= addition+1 can be seen as the result of adding 1 to the original data value stored in the sum memory address, and then re-assigning to the memory space corresponding to the sum memory address. The right side of the assignment operator "=" can be a constant, variable or expression, and will eventually assign the value to the variable on the left.

On the left side of the operator can only be variables, not numeric values, functions, expressions, etc. For example, the expression first-second=Third is an illegal program statement.

Python assignment operators have two types of assignments: single assignment and compound assignment.

For example, the sample1 = 10 assignment operator can assign the same value to multiple variables at the same time, in addition to assigning one value to the variable at a time. If we want multiple variables to have the same variable value at the same time, we can assign variable values together. For example, if you want variables first, second, and third to have values of 100, the assignment statement can be written as follows:

first= second = third = 100 when you want to assign values to multiple variables in the same line of program statements, you can separate variables with,"." For example, if you want the variable first to have a value of 10, the variable second to have a value of 20, and the variable third to have a value of 30, write the assignment statement as follows: first, second, third = 10, 20, and 30 python also allows ";."

To continuously write several different program statements to separate different expressions.

For example, the following two lines of program code:

result= 10

Index = 12 ";"can be used. Write the above two lines on the same line.

Please look at the following demonstration:

result= 10;

Index = 12 # concatenates two program statements or expressions with semicolons in one line

Exercise

The report card statistics assistant is again time to practice. The theme is to make a report card statistics program. Enter the names of 10 students and their scores in mathematics, English, and Chinese. Calculate the total score and average score and judge which grade belongs to A, B, C, and D according to the average score. 3.8.1 The sample program shows that this time, the students' scores are not inputted one by one, which is too time-consuming.

The author has established the scores.csv file in advance. The file contains the names of 10 students and their scores in mathematics, English, and Chinese. The topic requirements for this exercise are as follows:

(1) Read in a CSV file with the file name scores.csv

(2) Calculate the total score, average score, and grade (A, B, C, D). A: an average of 80 to 100 points b: an average of 60 to 79 points c: an average of 50 to 59 points d: an average of fewer than 50 points

(3) Output the student's name, total score, average score (reserved to one decimal place), and grade. CSV file.

The so-called open data refers to data that can be freely used and distributed. Although some open data require users to identify the data source and the owner, most open platforms for government data can obtain the data free of charge. These open data will be published on the network in common open formats.

If different applications want to exchange data, they must use a common data format. CSV format is one of them. The full name is Comma-Separated Values. Fields are separated by commas and are all plain text files like TXT files. They can be edited by text editors such as Notepad. CSV format is commonly used in spreadsheets and databases.

For example, Excel files can export data to CSV format or import CSV files for editing. Much Open Data on the network will also provide users with directly downloaded CSV format data. When you learn how to process CSV files, you can use these data for more analysis and application.

Python Built-in CSV module can process CSV files very easily. CSV module is a standard library module, which must be imported with import instruction before use. Let's look at the usage of the CSV module. Usage of the CSV module can read CSV file or write to CSV file. Before reading, you must first open the CSV file and then use the CSV.reader method to read the contents of the CSV file.

The code is as follows:

[get the module] csv # to load csv.py

With open ("furst.csv," encoding = "utf-8") ascsvfile:

open file specified as cssvfile

Reader = csv.reader (cssvfile)

```
# returns reader object

For row in reader:

#for loop reads data row by row
```

LOOPS

What Is a Loop?

We sometimes need some portion of our programs to repeat when a specific condition is satisfied. This is achieved using loops. As in the conditional statements, the loops also have blocks. In the if-else structure, the if block or the else block was executed depending on the condition. In loops, the loop block is repeatedly executed as long as the condition is satisfied. This means that the condition has to be modified inside the loop block so that the number of repetitions of a loop would be finite, otherwise the loop would become an infinite loop which makes our programs stuck.

The *while* loop

The general structure of a while loop is as follows:

while (condition):

commands in the

while block will

be executed until

the condition becomes

False

Let's analyze a simple while loop example as follows:

a=0

while a<20:

print ("Current value of a is", a)

a += 1

print ("The loop ended.")

```
Python 3.6.5 Shell                                          —    □    ×
File  Edit  Shell  Debug  Options  Window  Help
Python 3.6.5 (v3.6.5:f59c0932b4, Mar 28 2018, 16:07:46) [MSC v.1900 32 bit (Inte
1)] on win32
Type "copyright", "credits" or "license()" for more information.
>>>
== RESTART: C:/Users/machost/Desktop/Python examples/python_program_5_1.py ==
Current value of a is 0
Current value of a is 1
Current value of a is 2
Current value of a is 3
Current value of a is 4
Current value of a is 5
Current value of a is 6
Current value of a is 7
Current value of a is 8
Current value of a is 9
Current value of a is 10
Current value of a is 11
Current value of a is 12
Current value of a is 13
Current value of a is 14
Current value of a is 15
Current value of a is 16
Current value of a is 17
Current value of a is 18
Current value of a is 19
The loop ended.
>>>
                                                              Ln: 26  Col: 4
```

The value of *a* is set as 0 at the beginning. The commands in the while loop (again, an indented block) will be executed as if *a* is less than 20

(a<20). In the beginning a=0 therefore the command in the loop will execute. First, the print statement will print the current value of *a* as 0.

Then the expression a += 1 will increment *a* by one making the new value of *a* to be 1. Then the loop condition will be checked again. Since *a* is still less than 20, the command in the loop block will be executed also and the new value of a will be 2. This will continue until a=20. When a=20, the loop condition will be broken, and then looping will end. The last line which is after

49

the loop will be executed and the program will exit. The output of our program utilizing a while loop.

We increment the loop variable a so that at some point the loop will exit.

In the above example, we incremented it by one in each loop (a += 1). We can modify the loop variable per our need, not necessarily incrementing by 1.

For example, let's increment a by 5 in each loop:

```
Python 3.6.5 Shell                                          —  □  ×
File  Edit  Shell  Debug  Options  Window  Help
Python 3.6.5 (v3.6.5:f59c0932b4, Mar 28 2018, 16:07:46) [MSC v.1900 32 bit (In
tel)] on win32
Type "copyright", "credits" or "license()" for more information.
>>>
== RESTART: C:/Users/machost/Desktop/Python examples/python_program_5_2.py ==
Current value of a is 0
Current value of a is 5
Current value of a is 10
Current value of a is 15
The loop ended.
>>> |
                                                         Ln: 10  Col: 4
```

a=0

while a<20:

print ("Current value of a is", a)

```
a += 5
```

```
print ("The loop ended.")
```

The output of this program will show that a is incremented by 5 in each loop:

The same loop incrementing the value of a by 5

Note that *Current value of a is 20* is not executed as the a=20 breaks the loop condition (a<20) and the loop has existed before executing this command.

If we fail to make the loop condition False at some point, the loop continues forever and forms an infinite loop. For example, if we forget to increment the value of the loop variable, we form an infinite loop: a=0

```
while a<20:
```

```
print ("Current value of a is", a)
```

```
print ("The loop ended.")
```

Since the value of will not be updated, the loop will

continue printing

Current value of a is 0 forever. I have done the dangerous 105

```
Python 3.6.5 Shell                                              —  □  ×

File  Edit  Shell  Debug  Options  Window  Help

Current  value  of  a  is  0
Current  value  of  a  is  0
Current  value  of  a  is  0
Current  value  of  a  is  0
Current  value  of  a  is  0
Current  value  of  a  is  0
Current  value  of  a  is  0
Current  value  of  a  isTraceback  (most  recent  call  last):
  File  "C:/Users/machost/Desktop/Python  examples/python_program_5_3.py",  line  3,
  in  <module>
    print("Current  value  of  a  is",  a)
KeyboardInterrupt
>>>
                                                              Ln: 526  Col: 4
```

Note: Executed this program in IDLE (infinite loop WARNING: don't try at home, or you can try and just press CTRL together to force quit the IDLE prompt):

The infinite loop tried to print *Current value of a is 0* infinitely until I have beaten it by pressing Ctrl+C

Another possible situation where an infinite loop occurs is setting the loop condition incorrectly.

For example:

a=1

while a>0:

print("Current value of a is", a)

a += 1

print("The loop ended.")

Since the value of a will always be greater than 0, the loop condition will always be True and the loop will continue forever (until we press Ctrl+C).

```
Python 3.6.5 Shell                                        —    □    ×

File  Edit  Shell  Debug  Options  Window  Help
Current value of a is 168
Current value of a is 169
Current value of a is 170
Current value of a is 171
Current value of a is 172
Current value of a is 173
Current value of a is 174
Current value of a is 175
Current value of a is 176
Current value of a is 177
Current value of a is 178
Current value of a is 179
Current value of a is 180
Current value of a is Traceback (most recent call last):
  File "C:/Users/machost/Desktop/Python examples/python_program_5_4.py", line 3,
in <module>
    print("Current value of a is", a)
KeyboardInterrupt
>>>
                                                              Ln: 189  Col: 4
```

Another infinite loop beaten by Ctrl+C

Therefore, we should be extra careful about the loop conditions to avoid infinite loops.

The *break* and *continue* keywords.

The break and continue keywords are used for controlling the behavior of loops. When a break statement is executed in a loop, the loop exits immediately without checking the state of the loop variable: a=0

while a<11:

if a==5:

print("The break statement will be executed now.")

break

print("Current value of a is", a)

a += 1

print("Loop finished.")

The loop would print the values of a as 0,1...,10. However, when a=5, the condition of the if the statement becomes True and the commands inside the if the statement is executed, including the break statement.

Therefore, the loop ends immediately when a=5:

```
Python 3.6.5 Shell                                    —    □    ×
File  Edit  Shell  Debug  Options  Window  Help
Python 3.6.5 (v3.6.5:f59c0932b4, Mar 28 2018, 16:07:46) [MSC v.1900 32 bit (Inte
1)] on win32
Type "copyright", "credits" or "license()" for more information.
>>>
== RESTART: C:/Users/machost/Desktop/Python examples/python_program_5_5.py ==
Current value of a is 0
Current value of a is 1
Current value of a is 2
Current value of a is 3
Current value of a is 4
Current value of a is 5
The break statement will be executed now.
Loop finished.
>>>
                                                          Ln: 13  Col: 4
```

The break keyword broke the loop.

```
Python 3.6.5 Shell                                    —    □    ×
File  Edit  Shell  Debug  Options  Window  Help
Python 3.6.5 (v3.6.5:f59c0932b4, Mar 28 2018, 16:07:46) [MSC v.1900 32 bit (Inte
1)] on win32
Type "copyright", "credits" or "license()" for more information.
>>>
== RESTART: C:/Users/machost/Desktop/Python examples/python_program_5_6.py ==
Please enter the password:abcde
Incorrect password!! Please try again...
Please enter the password:12589
Incorrect password!! Please try again...
Please enter the password:12345
Correct password.
>>>
                                                          Ln: 11  Col: 4
```

We can also use the True keyword as the loop condition to
intentionally make an infinite loop and use the break statement
to control the loop as follows:

while True:

user_input=input("Please enter the password:")

if user_input == "12345":

print("Correct password.")

break

print("Incorrect password!! Please try

again...")

Since the loop condition is set as True, the while loop is expected to execute indefinitely. However, if the user enters the correct password, the commands in the if statement will execute breaking the infinite cycle. The loop continues until the correct password is entered.

```
Python 3.6.5 Shell                                      —  □  ×

File  Edit  Shell  Debug  Options  Window  Help
Python 3.6.5 (v3.6.5:f59c0932b4, Mar 28 2018, 16:07:46) [MSC v.1900 32 bit (Inte
1)] on win32
Type "copyright", "credits" or "license()" for more information.
>>>
== RESTART: C:/Users/machost/Desktop/Python examples/python_program_5_7.py ==
Current value of a is 0
Current value of a is 1
Current value of a is 2
Current value of a is 3
The commands under this point will be skipped.
The loop will continue with the next value.
Current value of a is 5
Current value of a is 6
Current value of a is 7
Current value of a is 8
Current value of a is 9
The loop ended.
>>>
                                                                Ln: 17  Col: 4
```

Another useful command used in conjunction with loops is the continue keyword. Its operation is similar to the break statement.

However, instead of finishing the loop, the continue command makes the program to skip the current iteration of the loop and continue with the next iteration:

```
a=0

while a<10:

if a==4:

a += 1

print("The commands under this point will be skipped.\nThe

The loop will continue with the next value.")

continue

print("Current value of a is", a)

a += 1

print("The loop ended.")
```

In this example, when a=4, the if block will be executed which contains a continue statement. The execution of the current loop will be skipped and continue with the next iteration:

continue statement skipped the loop at a=4

```
Python 3.6.5 Shell                                          —  □  ×

File  Edit  Shell  Debug  Options  Window  Help
Python 3.6.5 (v3.6.5:f59c0932b4, Mar 28 2018, 16:07:46) [MSC v.1900 32 bit (Inte
l)] on win32
Type "copyright", "credits" or "license()" for more information.
>>>
== RESTART: C:/Users/machost/Desktop/Python examples/python_program_5_8.py ==
The 0th element of the list is: 1
The 1th element of the list is: 2
The 2th element of the list is: 4
The 3th element of the list is: 5
The 4th element of the list is: 8
The 5th element of the list is: 9
The 6th element of the list is: 11
The 7th element of the list is: 15
>>> |

                                                        Ln: 13  Col: 4
```

The *for* loop

Another type of loop in Python is the for loop. The for loop enables us to sweep over a list, tuple, or dictionary structure easily without the need for managing the loop variable. In order to observe the ease provided by the for loop, let's first try to sweep over a list using the while loop:

my_list=[1,2,4,5,8,9,11,15]

i=0 # The loop variable

while i<len(my_list):

print("The {}th element of the list is:

{}".format(i, my_listChapteri]))

i += 1

58

Here, we defined a loop variable i and swept it from 0 to the number which is (length of my_list -1) and printed the value of i th element in each iteration:

Sweeping over the elements of a list using a while loop and managing a loop variable

The same program can be re-written using the for loop as follows: my_list=[1,2,4,5,8,9,11,15]

for the member in my_list:

print("The current element of the list is:", member)

```
Python 3.6.5 Shell                                    —    □    X

File  Edit  Shell  Debug  Options  Window  Help
Python 3.6.5 (v3.6.5:f59c0932b4, Mar 28 2018, 16:07:46) [MSC v.1900 32 bit (Inte
1)] on win32
Type "copyright", "credits" or "license()" for more information.
>>>
== RESTART: C:/Users/machost/Desktop/Python examples/python_program_5_9.py ==
The current element of the list is: 1
The current element of the list is: 2
The current element of the list is: 4
The current element of the list is: 5
The current element of the list is: 8
The current element of the list is: 9
The current element of the list is: 11
The current element of the list is: 15
>>>
                                                              Ln: 13  Col: 4
```

```
Python 3.6.5 Shell                                                    —   □   ×

File  Edit  Shell  Debug  Options  Window  Help
Python 3.6.5 (v3.6.5:f59c0932b4, Mar 28 2018, 16:07:46) [MSC v.1900 32 bit (Inte
l)] on win32
Type "copyright", "credits" or "license()" for more information.
>>>
== RESTART: C:/Users/machost/Desktop/Python examples/python_program_5_10.py ==
H
e
l
l
o
>>> |
                                                                    Ln: 10  Col: 4
```

Sweeping over the list elements using the for loop, the general structure of a for loop is s follows:

for member in list:

Commands in the loop (typically using the current member of the loop) We can also sweep over strings using the for loop:

my_string="Hello"

for current_char in my_string:

print(current_char)

The for loop iterates the string's each element (character) and prints on the screen:

```
Python 3.6.5 Shell                                    —    □    X

File  Edit  Shell  Debug  Options  Window  Help
Python 3.6.5 (v3.6.5:f59c0932b4, Mar 28 2018, 16:07:46) [MSC v.1900 32 bit (Inte
l)] on win32
Type "copyright", "credits" or "license()" for more information.
>>>
== RESTART: C:/Users/machost/Desktop/Python examples/python_program_5_11.py ==
0 1 2 3 4 5 6 7 8 9
>>> |



                                                                    Ln: 6  Col: 4
```

Sweeping a string using a for loop.

The *range()* function

The for loop can also be used to iterate over tuples and dictionaries but this is rarely used. On the other hand, we can also form a number sequence using a built -in the function called range() and iterate over this sequence using the for loop. The usage of the range() function is as follows:

sequence=range(start, stop, step(optional))

Let's form a sequence using the range function and print it:
sequence=range(0,10)

print(*sequence)

Note that we used the * operator here to split the values of the sequence for printing on the screen (remember that we used the * operator in strings too). Also, note that the last value specified in the range function is not included in the sequence:

The output sequence of the range function

We can iterate over the elements of a range() function as follows: for i in range(0,10,2):

print(i)

```
Python 3.6.5 Shell                                        —    □    ×
File  Edit  Shell  Debug  Options  Window  Help
Python 3.6.5 (v3.6.5:f59c0932b4, Mar 28 2018, 16:07:46) [MSC v.1900 32 bit (Inte
1)] on win32
Type "copyright", "credits" or "license()" for more information.
>>>
== RESTART: C:/Users/machost/Desktop/Python examples/python_program_5_12.py ==
0
2
4
6
8
>>> |
                                                                    Ln: 10  Col: 4
```

In this program, we created a sequence using the range() function which goes from 0 to 9 with step=2, therefore the sequence returned by range(0,10,2) is 0,2,4,6,8. Let's try this in Python:

Elements of the sequence returned by the range(0,10,2) function are printed using a for loop.

That's all about the loops in Python. Please try to write the programs given in the exercises below before continuing to the next chapter where we will see writing our own functions in Python.

Exercises

1. The factorial of a number n is defined as n!=n.(n-1).(n-2)...2.1. For example, 6!=6.5.4.3.2.1=720. Please write a program that asks for an integer from the user and calculates and prints the factorial of that number.

2. Write a program that calculates and prints the sum of the first 100 positive integers.

3. Write a program that will ask for the grades of 20 students and will calculate the average of these grades.

4. Write a program that will calculate the greatest common divisor of two numbers entered by the user.

Beginner's Guide to Python Programming

5. Write a program that will print the integers from n to 0 in the reverse order such as if n=6, the program will print 6,5,4,3,2,1,0. The value of n will be entered by the user.

INTERACTING WITH PYTHON

Finally, any application you fabricate interfaces with the PC and the information implanted. The emphasis is on the information in light of the fact that there is no rhyme or reason to have an application without information. Any application you use deals with the information somehow. The abbreviation CRUD sums up what most applications do:

• Create

• Read

• Update

• Delete

Utilize the order line for your potential benefit

To begin Python from an order brief, type Python and press Enter. Be that as it may, that is not everything you can do. You can likewise give extra data to change the manner in which Python works:

Alternatives:

A choice or order line choice starts with a short sign followed by at least one letter. For instance, on the off chance that you need assistance with Python, type Python - h and press Enter. You see extra data about utilizing Python on the order line.

Document Name:

Providing an info record name advises Python to stack that document and run it. You can run any example application from the download code by giving the filename containing the info model. For instance, assume you have a model called SayHello.py. To run this model, type Python SayHello.py and press Enter.

Contentions: Additional data can be acknowledged by an application as a contribution to control its execution. This extra data is called contention.

Most decisions don't bode well at this point. For instance, - s is an alternate choice from - S. Python alternatives are

- b: Add admonitions to the yield when your application utilizes some Python highlights, including str (bytes_instance), str (bytearray_ occurrence), and coordinating bytes or bytearray with str ().

- bb: add mistakes to the yield when your application utilizes some Python highlights, for example, str (bytes_instance), str (bytearray_ occasion), and coordinating bytes or bytearray with str ().

- B: Do not type .py or .pyco records when you play out a module import.

- C cmd: Use the data gave by cmd to begin a program. This choice additionally advises Python to stop handling on the remainder of the data as alternatives (they are prepared as a significant aspect of the order).

- d: dispatches the debugger (used to search for mistakes in your application).

- E: Ignore all Python condition factors, for example, PYTHONPATH, used to design Python use.

- h: Displays help on choices and factors in the fundamental screen condition. Python consistently stops in the wake of playing out this assignment without taking any kind of action so you can see the assistance data.

- I: Python power to let you assess the code intelligently subsequent to running a content. Power a brief regardless of whether stdin (the default input gadget) doesn't give off an impression of being a terminal.

- m mod: Launches the module determined by mod as a content.

- O: somewhat enhances the produced bytecode (makes it quicker).

- OO: Performs extra streamlining by erasing report strings.

- q: advises Python not to print form and copyright messages at the intuitive beginning.

- s: power Python not to add the client's site registry to sys.path (a variable that discloses to Python where to discover the modules).

- S: Do not dispatch "import site" at startup. Utilizing this choice implies that Python won't search for ways that may contain the necessary modules.

- u: Allow unbuffered bitstreams for stdout (standard yield) and stderr (classic blunder) gadgets. The stdin gadget is still cushioned.

- v: Put Python in the full mode with the goal that you can see all the import guidelines. Utilizing this choice on numerous occasions expands the degree of verbosity.

- W arg: Allow Python to show little alarms by decreasing the alarm level. Legitimate arg values are:

• Action

- Message

- Classification

- Module

- Lineno

- x: overlook the main line of a source code record, which permits utilizing of non-Unix types of #! Cmd.

- X pick: Defines an alternative explicit to the execution. (The documentation for your Python form examines these alternatives assuming any.)

Use Python Environment Variables to your Advantage

Condition factors are explicit boundaries that are a piece of the order line or terminal condition of the working framework. They are utilized to arrange Python reliably. Condition factors perform vast numbers of similar alternatives exercises set when beginning Python.

Most working frameworks permit you to briefly set nature factors by designing them during a particular meeting or arranging them forever as a significant aspect of the operating framework arrangement. The most effective method to play out this errand relies upon the working framework. For instance, the Define order can be embraced when working with Windows.

The utilization of condition factors is valuable when you have to design Python similarly all the time. The Python condition factors are recorded beneath:

PYTHONCASEOK = x: Python constrains you to overlook the situation while investigating the import guidelines. This is a Windows interface just for factors.

PYTHONDEBUG = x: plays out a similar movement as the - d choice.

PYTHONDONTWRITEBYTECODE = x: plays out a similar movement as an alternative - B.

PYTHONFAULTHANDLER = x: Python powers Python following to bomb lethally.

PYTHONHASHSEED = arg: decides the seed esteem that is utilized to produce hash esteems for different sorts of information. At the point when this variable is indiscriminate,

Python uses an irregular incentive to engender the hashes of the DateTime, str, and byte objects. The full legitimate range is from 0 to 4294967295.

Utilize a particular seed an incentive to create an anticipated hash incentive for testing purposes.

PYTHONHOME = arg: sets the default search way utilized by Python to scan for modules.

PYTHONINSPECT = x: plays out a similar movement as the - I choice.

PYTHONIOENCODING = arg: indicate the encoding [: errors], (for example, utf-8) utilized for stderr, stdin and stdout gadgets.

PYTHONNOUSERSITE = plays out a similar action as the - s choice.

PYTHONOPTIMIZE = x: plays out a similar action as the - O choice.

PYTHONPATH = arg: gives a comma-isolated rundown of catalogs (;) to look for modules.

PYTHONSTARTUP = arg: characterizes the record name that will be executed when the Python application is begun. This condition variable doesn't have default esteem.

PYTHONUNBUFFERED = x: plays out a similar activity as the - u choice.

PYTHONVERBOSE = x: plays out a similar movement as the - v alternative.

PYTHONWARNINGS = arg: plays out a similar movement as the - W choice.

Enter a request

Subsequent to propelling the Python order line rendition, you can start to type orders. Utilizing orders permits you to perform errands, test your thoughts for composing your application, and find more Python data. Using the order line gives you a hands-on understanding of how Python functions - subtleties that can be covered up by an intuitive improvement condition (IDE, for example, IDLE. The accompanying areas permit you to begin utilizing the order line.

Instruct the PC

Python, similar to some other programming language, relies upon the orders. An order is basically a phase inside a method. When working with Python, an order, similar to print (), is the same: a stage inside a methodology.

For the PC to comprehend what to do, it issues at least one order perceived by Python. Python makes an interpretation of these orders into guidelines comprehended by the PC; so observe the outcome. An order like print () can show the outcomes on the screen for guaranteed results. Be that as it may, Python is good with a wide range of orders, some of which show no outcomes on the screen, yet at the same time, keep on accomplishing something significant. As you travel through the book, you use orders to play out a wide range of errands. Every one of these undertakings will assist you with accomplishing an objective, just as the means of a technique.

Tell the PC you're finished

Sooner or later, the made technique closes. When toasting, the procedure closes when you get done with buttering. IT systems work in a similar way. They have a state of takeoff and appearance. When entering orders, the endpoint of a particular advance is the Enter key.

You press Enter to leave the PC alone mindful that you are going to type the order. All through the book, you will realize that Python offers a few different ways to demonstrate that a stage, a gathering of steps, or even a total application is finished. Regardless of how the undertaking is done, PC programs consistently have a different beginning stage and breakpoint.

See the outcome

You currently realize that a request is a stage in a strategy and that each request has a different beginning and endpoint.

Additionally, order gatherings and whole applications likewise have various beginnings and endings points.

GETTING STARTED; PYTHON TIPS AND TRICKS

We are going to look at some of the tips and tricks that will help you to get started with Python, along with how we can work with web scraping and debugging some of our programs as well.

Let's get started with this one to help us get started and finalize how good our codes can be.

Web Scraping

Imagine for a moment that we are going to pull up a large amount of data from many websites, and we want to be able to do this at a very fast rate.

How would we be able to go through this without having to manually go through each of the websites that we have and gathering the data in this manner?

This is where the process of web scraping is going to come into play.

Web scraping is going to be used by companies in order to collect a large amount of information from websites.

But why does someone want to go through and collect all of this data, in such large amounts, from these websites in the first place?

There are a lot of reasons for this, and some of them are going to include the following:

• Price comparison: Some of the different services that are out there, such as ParseHub, will work with this process in order to collect data from websites for online shopping and then can use this in order to compare prices of similar products.

• Email address gathering: We can use the process of web scraping in order to help with marketing.

This can help us to collect the email IDs that come with customers and then send out bulk emails to these individuals as well.

• Research and development: Web scraping is going to be used to help a company collect a lot of data from websites.

We can then analyze this and use it to finish our surveys and to help out with research and development.

• Job listing: Details regarding openings of jobs, interviews, and more can be collected from a variety of websites and then we can list them in one place in order to make them easier for the user to access

Web scraping is going to be more of an automated method that we can use in order to get a huge amount of data from any website that we choose.

The data that we are able to get out of these websites will be unstructured. And this web scraping helps a company to collect all of this data and then will ensure that they are able to store it in a structured form.

There are a variety of methods that we are able to use in order to scrape these websites that we want, including online Services, writing out some of your own codes, and APIs.

Talking about whether or not scraping of this kind is seen as legal or not, it can depend on what the website says. Some websites are fine with this, and some are not.

You can check with each website to figure out whether they are fine with it, and if they are, you are able to continue on with your web scraping tools and gather up the information that you need.

Since we are talking about Python here, we are going to take some time to see how we are able to use Python to help out with web scraping. But this brings up the reasons why we would want to work with Python to help out with this process rather than working with some of the other coding languages that are out there.

Some of the features that come with Python and can make it more suitable for web scraping will include:

• It is easy to use: The code that you are able to use along with Python is going to be simple. This ensures that any of the codes that you want to use for web scraping will not be as messy to work with and can be easy to use.

• A large library collection: There are a lot of libraries that work with data science and web scraping that are also compatible with what the Python language is able to do.

These include options like Pandas, Matplotlib, and NumPy.

This is why you will find that the Python language is going to be suitable for web scraping and even for some of the other manipulations that you want to do with the extracted data.

• Dynamically typed: This is something in Python where you will not need to go through and define all of the types of data that you are using with our variables.

Instead, you are able just to use these variables wherever you would like. This is going to save a lot of time when it comes to working on the codes and can make your job faster than ever.

• The syntax of Python is going to be easy to understand the syntax that we are able to see with Python is easy to understand, mainly because the statements that come with this are going to be written in English. It is going to be expressive and easy to read, and the indentations will make it easier for us to figure out between the different parts of the code.

• A small line of code is able to handle some large tasks. Web scraping is a process that we are going to use in order to save some time.

And with Python, you are able to write out a small amount of code in order to get some of the big tasks that you would like to accomplish done.

This is going to save you time not only when it comes to figuring out the important data that comes in that website, but can also help you to save time when you would like to write out the codes.

• Community: At times, when you are a beginner, you are going to find that there are parts of the code that are hard to work with and are not going to go as smoothly as you had hoped in the process.

This is where you will find the Python language to be healthy.

If you get stuck while writing out some of your code, you will like that the Python community is going to help you to answer your questions and get things done on the code in no time.

Now that we know some of the benefits that come with Python, especially the ones that are going to help us to handle some of the web scrapings that we want to do, it is time for us to take things to the next step and look at how the process of web scraping is going to work.

When you run out the code that you want to work within web scraping, you will find that there is a request that is sent out to the URL.

Then there is going to be a response sent back from that request, and then the server is able to send the data and allows you a chance to read the page, whether it is XML or HTML at the time.

The code is then able to go through and parse the XML or HTML page, find the data, and takes it out.

The location where you are going to find this data when it is extracted will depend on what you told the code to do.

Often it is going to be moved over to a database so that you are able to search through it later and learn more from it as well.

There are going to be a few simple steps that you are able to take to make something to help us go through the process of extracting the data with the help of web scraping in Python.

The steps that will help you to use Python to help with web scraping include:

- Find the URL that you would like to scrape in the first place.

- Inspect the page that you are planning on using.

- Find the data that is on the page that you would like to extract.

- Write out the code that you would like to use with the help of Python in order to complete this process.

- Run the code that you just wrote and then extract out the data that you would like to use.

- Store the data in the format that would be the most helpful for you in the process.

There are also a few options that you are able to use when it is time to work on the process of web scraping.

As we know, Python is already able to be used for a lot of different types of applications, and there are going to be a ton of libraries with Python that is going to be used for different purposes.

There are a few libraries that work the best when it comes to working with the process of data web scraping will include:

1. Selenium: This is going to be a web testing library.

It is going to be used to help automate some of the activities that are found on your browser.

2. BeautifulSoup: This is going to be one of those packages that you are able to use with Python to help us to parse HTML and XML documents.

It is also able to create parse trees that can help us to extract the data in an easy manner.

3. Pandas: This is one of the best libraries to rely on when it is time to handle any kind of work that you would like in data analysis and data science.

Pandas are often going to be used to help out with any of the data analysis and the data manipulation that you would like.

When it comes to web scraping, you will find that Pandas is going to be used in order to extract the data and then get it stored in the right format in the way that you would like along the way.

There are many times when a company is going to try and gather up data from other websites and from many other sources.

This is one of the first steps that is going to be found when we are working with data analysis and using that information to improve a business through their customers, the industry, or from the other competition out there.

But going through and gathering all of that data in a manual manner is going to take too long, and can be really hard to work with as well.

And with the large amounts of data that are being used and generated on a daily basis, it is no wonder that so many companies are working with processes like web scraping to handle all of the work in a timely manner as well.

When we work with web scraping and do some of the codings that are necessary with the help of Python, we will find that we are able to get through the information in a fast manner and get it stored in the right place for our needs, without having to do all of the work manually.

This can make the process of data analysis much easier overall and will ensure that we are able to see some of the results that we want with this as well.

And with some of the right Python algorithms and codes, we can get data scraping done in no time.

DEBUGGING

Debugging

Developers always discover themselves in situations in which the code they have written is not functioning quite well. When this happens, a developer adjusts their "codes" by run-time-instrumentation, examining and carrying out "code" to create solutions to which part of the implementation does not go along with the presumptions of the way the "code" must be accurately working. And due to the fact that debugging is so simple. All developers cherish it.

Debugging tools

There are several debugging implements, certain of which designed into IDEs such as PyCharm and different alone applications. The below list always involves nondependent implements that can be used in whatever development area.

PDB is a debugger included within the Python Quality library and is the one majority of developers initially use when making attempts to look into their projects.

Web-PDB provides a network-based UI for PDB to enable it to be more understandable what's happening in the process of checking your running code.

Wdb makes use of WebSockets to help you to eliminate running Python code from a network browser.

Pdb Module

The singular thing we are to talk about here is PDB. In software development language, the term debugging is usually made use to process positioning and correcting the mistake in a program.

The PDB has a useful command-line associate. It is inserted at the period of running of Python script by making use of –m switch.

In this initial instance, we will check at making use of PDB in its easy form. Add the below code at the position where you want fragment into the debugger:

```
import pdb; pdb.set_trace()
```

At the stage when the above line runs, Python halts and holds on for you to instruct it after. You will notice a (PDB) message. It described you are currently halted in the instinctive debugger and can input a command.

Starting in Python 3.7, there is another method to gain entrance to the debugger. PEP 553 gives meaning to the designed function breakpoint (), which makes entering the debugger simple and steady:

```
breakpoint()
```

In addition, breakdown() will bring in PDB and call PDB .set_trace () as indicated above.

Nevertheless, making use of breakpoint () is adaptable and helps you to curb debugging attitude through its API and make use of the environment variable PYTHONBREAKPOINT. For instance, adjusting PYTHONBREAKPOINT=0 in your surrounding will totally disable breakpoint (), therefore stopping debugging. Are you using Python 3.7 or another? If yes, I implore you to make use of breakpoint() in place of PDB.set_trace().

You can as well break into the debugger, lest altering the origin and making use of breakpoint() or PDB.set_trace, by executing Python directly from the command-line and moving the alternative −m PDB. In case your application gives room for command-line arguments, offer them as you often would after the folder name.

For instance:

Shell:

```
$ python3 -m pdb app.py arg1 arg2
```

To additionally find the way debugger works, let's inscribe a Python module (fact.py) as below:

```python
def fact(x):
    f = 1
    for i in range(1,x+1):
        print (i)
        f = f * i
    return f
if __name__=="__main__":
    print ("factorial of 3=",fact(3))
```

Start debugging this module from the command line. In this example, the running stops at the initial line in the code by displaying (->) to its left and presenting a debugger prompt (PDB).

```
C:\python36>python -m pdb fact.py
> c:\python36\fact.py(1)<module>()
-> def fact(x):
(Pdb)
```

Debugging Commands

Fundamentally, a debugger implement gives you a technique to, an instance, unlock the application in a particular place in order

88

to be able to look at your variables, call stack or not considering what it is necessary to see, set limitation breakpoints, and move via the origin code a line at each time and so on. It is similar to searching segment by segment to identify the problem.

There is a designed debugger in Python, named PDB. It is an important value with a command-line combination that carries out the internal work. It possesses every debugger property that you will need, nevertheless if you wish to propel it a bit, you can expand it by making use of ipdb, which will give the debugger with properties from IPython.

```
import pdb; pdb.set_trace()
```

The very clear method to apply PDB is to call it the code you are running:

As soon as the translator gets to this line, you will receive a command prompt on the end where you are executing the program. It is a normal Python prompt, however with certain recent commands.

List(l)

On the uncertainty that it is necessary to check a different part of the code, this command has arguments for the initial and the final lines to display. If you give simply the figure of the original line, you will have the opportunity to see the code around the line you have assigned.

Up(p) and down(d)

Up(p) and down(d) are the two commands needed to survey within the call stack. With the help of the above commands, you can see, the person calling the present function, for instance, or why the translator is heading a particular way.

Step(s) and next(n)

More important couple of commands, step (s) and next (n) help you to keep the running of the application step by step. The special distinction between the two is that next(n) will simply move to the following line of the present function, despite having a call for a different function, nevertheless, step (s) will go further in a situation like this.

Break(b)

The command (b) helps you to structure several breakpoints without altering the code. It requires additional explanations; therefore, I will go further below.

In this image is a bright summary of other PDB commands:

Command	What it does
args (a)	Gets you the argument list of the current function
continue (c) or (cont)	Creates a breakpoint in the program execution (requires parameters)
help (h)	Provides a list of commands or help for a certain command
jump (j)	Jumps to the next line to be executed
list (l)	Prints the source code around the current line
Expression (p)	Evaluates the expression in the current context and prints its value
pp (pp)	Pretty-prints the value of the expression
quit or exit (q)	Aborts the program
return (r)	Continues the execution until the current function returns

UNDERSTANDING MACHINE LEARNING

We will explain additional machine learning models and algorithms in simple terms – with a goal for the reader to be able to understand them at a high level and know when to apply them given the nature of the data and their data science use case.

At the highest level, machine learning models can be classified into three categories:

1)   Supervised Machine Learning Models
2)   Unsupervised Machine Learning Models
3)   Deep Learning Models

Supervised Machine Learning Models

In the case of supervised machine learning models, the model is provided some direction in terms of how to classify the data and it uses those instructions to learn before making its predictions. The house sales example that we used in the previous chapter, was an example of supervised learning as we told the model what the different types of houses were and even which house features have an impact on the sales price. We then split the data set into training and test sets that the model used to make its prediction.

Examples of supervised machine learning models include:

1) Regression analysis
2) Classification analysis

Regression analysis

In the case of regression analysis, given several factors, the model is expected to predict a number. In the case of the house sales price example, the model considered several house features to predict the house sales price. Note that the above was an example of **linear regression** where there is a straight-line correlation between the dependent variable (e.g. house sales price) and independent variables (e.g. house type, number of garages, etc.).

There are certain situations where that straight-line correlation does not exist and typically in those situations, **polynomial regression** analysis is used – or a curved line instead of a straight line.

In other words, all the machine learning model is doing when performing regression analysis is trying to fit a line between scattered data points to find a correlation between independent and dependent variables. That can be illustrated visually as follows:

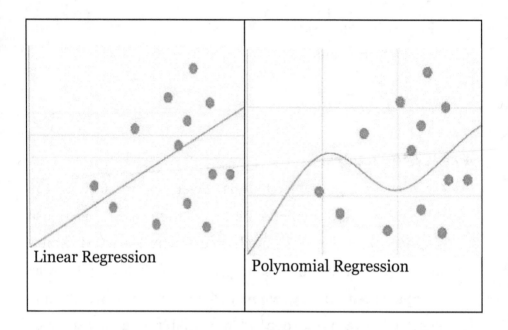

Linear Regression

Polynomial Regression

Other real-world examples of where regression analysis is used in the finance industry predicting stock price based on historical and market trends as well as in the retail industry where certain product prices are often predictable based on seasonality and time of the year e.g. clothing, outdoor patio, and gardening products.

Classification analysis

In the case of classification analysis, the machine learning model predicts the category for an object based on its features. So the main difference between the classification model and regression model is that the classification model is categorizing the objects and the regression model is predicting a number associated with an object.

Like regression analysis, since classification analysis is a supervised model, it will need to be provided labeled data with instructions to learn before it can make its predictions. If house sales data example in the previous chapter were a classification problem, the model would have been given house sales data without the house type and the model would have been asked to predict the house type (e.g. detached, semi-detached or townhome) based on the different features included in the dataset.

Other real-world examples where classification algorithm can be used include:

1) Classifying insurance applicant into different risk categories based on their health data
2) Categorizing call center calls as potential escalations, based on language and sentiment used
3) Categorizing incoming emails based on specific parameters

Unsupervised Machine Learning Models

Unsupervised models are basically like intelligent but unsupervised children – who are given a whole bunch of data but without a lot of direction or labeling of the data. The models then assess this data and draw conclusions. These conclusions continue to be refined as more data is provided to the model.

Examples of unsupervised machine learning models include:

1) Clustering
2) Dimension Reduction
3) Association Learning

Clustering

is, as the name suggests, like the classification model above where it defines clusters of similar objects but the main difference being that the model is not given any pre-defined categories to label the data with. It comes up with them on its own. As an example, imagine the model being asked to classify different kinds of unlabeled data – some data loosely fits in the time category, some data fits in the geographical category and some data is not fitting either of these dimensions and instead is grouped in the general data cluster as illustrated below:

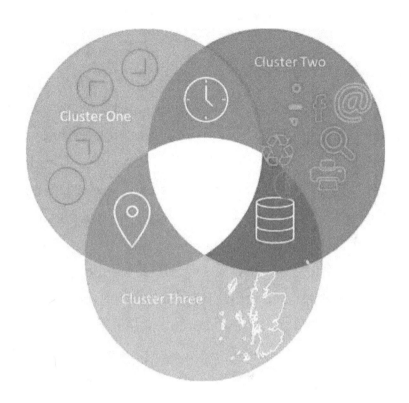

Real-world examples of clustering include detecting anomalies in cancer research based on cancerous cell properties as well as fraud detection based on irregular insurance claims or financial investment patterns in case of money laundering.

K-means algorithm is a popular algorithm in Python that is an example of clustering. Basically, the algorithm finds its nearest K neighbors that have similar properties – with K defining the number of neighbors you are pre-setting the model to find.

Dimension Reduction

is another example of an unsupervised machine learning model that takes a set of features of different objects and tries to categorize them to a higher degree of categories. Think of the Netflix algorithm to classify incoming movies and TV shows – it typically will roll up the different types of content to several high-level categories automatically like action, horror, or comedy. As new content gets added to the platform, the algorithm will further refine itself to cluster the movies more accurately. In certain cases, certain content on Netflix may fit multiple clusters. For example, a vampire movie with a lot of action can likely be in both the action and horror clusters.

Association Learning

is a more sophisticated form of unsupervised machine learning model that is learning from customer behavior and recommending new products and services to you based on your prior purchasing habits. These types of systems are often called recommender systems that associate client profiles with the product clusters and based on that generate recommendations. To extend the Netflix example, once the model has built clusters of different online viewable content, it associates the content with your prior viewing habits and recommends new movies and

TV shows to you that fit the categories you most often watch. The same logic applies to when Amazon recommends new books or products to you each time you log in.

Deep Learning

If you have ever heard the terms machine learning and deep learning interchangeably, I am here to tell you that they are not the same. Deep learning is an advanced form of machine learning where you combine several machine learning models in a network, often called a neural network, to arrive at a final conclusion or decision.

The reason why it is called 'deep learning', is based on how deep the neural network goes or how many nodes are part of the network – with each node representing a decision point or recommendation from an interconnecting model.

The neural network can be made more sophisticated by applying different weighting to different decision points or nodes and this weighting gets adjusted over time as the model becomes smarter by learning from more experience, trial and error, and more data provided to it. One example of this could be when you are looking for another job, when you are early in your career, you may put a higher weight on salary. However, as you gain more experience, you may start to add more weight to other aspects like work-life balance, benefits, and career progression opportunities. A sample neural network is illustrated below as an example:

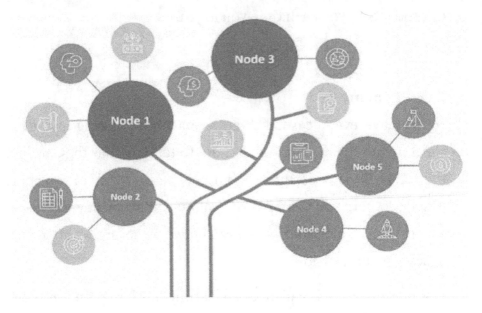

Popular deep learning Python libraries include:

1) TensorFlow

2) Keras

3) PyTorch

TensorFlow

is an open-source framework and API for programming deep learning neural networks and can be imported as a library in Python. It is capable of working with large data sets and is very efficient in data processing – that is why it is gaining a lot of popularity in data science and academic communities.

Keras

can run on top of the TensorFlow framework but is more suitable for smaller datasets and rapid prototyping. You will see it mostly in use when you are experimenting with neural networks in development and traversing the nodes of the neural networks as part of the trial and error process in teaching the model.

PyTorch

is most commonly used for natural language processing and was developed by Facebook. What is Natural Language Processing (NLP) you ask? It is a way for the machine learning models to interpret human language and process that as input into their algorithm. For example, instead of providing the model if-then-else conditions and code as in the previous chapter, you can ask the model questions in a human language like, "What would be my predicted house price based on the square footage?" and the model returns the prediction after running the question through the algorithm. Think of AI devices like Amazon's Alexa and Google Home. Those are examples of Natural Language Processing.

PYTHON CONCEPTS AT INTERMEDIATE LEVEL

This is a remarkably simple method to get going with Python. You'll love how easy such scripting will be about how many various systems can function. It's there. Quick enough to read by the novice after mastering any of the techniques, but also has the ability you want to function in the language of programming. It has the best of all worlds and is also one of the best computer languages—things to select from on the market.

Recursion in Python

A recursive function is a function that is described in self-referential words. It implies that the method continues naming itself while repeating its actions until those terms are fulfilled to produce a response. Both recursive functions have a standard two-part framework: base case & recursive case. To display this structure, let's compose a recursive measurement function n! : Disintegrate the current problem into simplified examples. That's the recursive case:

1. Decompose the initial query into simplified examples. That's the corrective situation:

```
n! = n x (n-1) x (n-2) x (n-3) ···· x 3 x 2 x 1
n! = n x (n-1)!
```

2. Because the real issue is separated into progressively less complicated, these sub-problems should gradually get so straightforward that they're being resolved with little differentiation. It is the fundamental situation:

```
n! = n x (n-1)!
n! = n x (n-1) x (n-2)!
n! = n x (n-1) x (n-2) x (n-3)!
.

.
n! = n x (n-1) x (n-2) x (n-3) ···· x 3!
n! = n x (n-1) x (n-2) x (n-3) ···· x 3 x 2!
n! = n x (n-1) x (n-2) x (n-3) ···· x 3 x 2 x 1!
```

Now, 1! It's indeed our base case, so it is equivalent to 1. Recursive approximation function n! By Python enacted:

```python
def factorial_recursive(n):
    # Base case: 1! = 1
    if n == 1:
        return 1

    # Recursive case: n! = n * (n-1)!
    else:
        return n * factorial_recursive(n-1)
```

```
>>> factorial_recursive(5)
120
```

Behind the curtains, a specific benchmark (usually contains the utilized resources) is inserted in the request stack before the specific case is reached. Therefore the stack continues to relax as every call yields its outcomes:

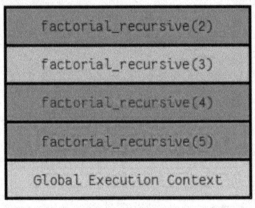

5*4*3*2!

Growing Call Stack

State management

Please remember when interacting with recursive functions, every other recursive call will have its own implementation background, and you have to hold a state throughout recursion:

- Link every recursive call via the state such that the present incarnation is in the operating context of the current call

- Hold the global space

A presentation will explain things. Let us just estimate 1 + 2 + 3 +4...... 10 by recursion. The condition we will hold is (current figure, which we have added up until now).

That's how to do so by using increasing recursive call (e.g., forwarding the latest modified status as arguments to every recursive call):

```python
def sum_recursive(current_number, accumulated_sum):
    # Base case
    # Return the final state
    if current_number == 11:
        return accumulated_sum

    # Recursive case
    # Thread the state through the recursive call
    else:
        return sum_recursive(current_number + 1, accumulated_sum + current_number)
```

Python   >>>

```python
# Pass the initial state
>>> sum_recursive(1, 0)
55
```

function i.e. sum_recursive(current_number, accumulated_sum)

Initial State
$S_1 (1, 0)$

Base case

if

Recursive case

S_1 (1, 0)

function

S_2 (2, 1)

function

S_3 (3, 3)

function

Final State
$S_n (11, 55)$

Control flow with threaded state

So this is how you calm the situation in global scope:

```python
# Global mutable state
current_number = 1
accumulated_sum = 0


def sum_recursive():
    global current_number
    global accumulated_sum
    # Base case
    if current_number == 11:
        return accumulated_sum
    # Recursive case
    else:
        accumulated_sum = accumulated_sum + current_number
        current_number = current_number + 1
        return sum_recursive()
```

```
>>> sum_recursive()
55
```

Recursive Data Structures

If it can be represented in a miniature version of its own, a data structure is recursive. A list is a resource management instance. Let us explain. Presume that you can only get a blank list available, and you can only do this procedure:

```
# Return a new list that is the result of
# adding element to the head (i.e. front) of input_list
def attach_head(element, input_list):
    return [element] + input_list
```

You may create any list using a blank list as well as the attached head process. Let us just create [1, 46, -31, "hello"], for instance:

```
attach_head(1,                              # Will return [1, 46,
        attach_head(46,                     # Will return [46, -3:
                attach_head(-31,            # Will return [-31, "I
                        attach_head("hello", []))))  # Will return ["hello'
```

```
[1, 46, -31, 'hello']
```

```
attach_head(1,  attach_head(46,  attach_head(-31, ["hello"])
```

Starting with a null list, a certain list can be generated using the attach head function iteratively, as well as the list structure can, therefore, be described recursively as:

```
        +---- attach_head(element, smaller list)
list = +
        +---- empty list
```

Recursion could also be seen as a structure of an auto-referential element. We add a feature to an argument and afterward transfer the outcome on to further use of this function, respectively. Formulating attach head amongst itself frequently is just the same as calling attach head again and again.

Perhaps the only recidivist data set is Collection. Set, tree, dictionary, etc. are other instances.

Recursive file systems and recursive functions fall hand in hand like milk and butter. The recursive function structure will also be based on the feedback by specifying the recursive database schema.

Let me show this by recurrently measuring the amount of each the components of a list:

```python
def list_sum_recursive(input_list):
    # Base case
    if input_list == []:
        return 0

    # Recursive case
    # Decompose the original problem into simpler instances of the same problem
    # by making use of the fact that the input is a recursive data structure
    # and can be defined in terms of a smaller version of itself
    else:
        head = input_list[0]
        smaller_list = input_list[1:]
        return head + list_sum_recursive(smaller_list)
```

Python   >>>

```
>>> list_sum_recursive([1, 2, 3])
6
```

Fibonacci Sequence

The Fibonacci numbers were initially conceived as the pattern of the development of rabbit species by Italian mathematician Fibonacci in the 13th century. Fibonacci assumed that the number of couples of rabbits raised in each of the twice preceding years is equal to the number of couples of rabbits raised through one pair in the first year.

He specified the recurrence ratio to track the number of rabbits raised in the nth years

A recursive function to accumulate the Fibonacci number

```python
def fibonacci_recursive(n):
    print("Calculating F", "(", n, ")", sep="", end=", ")

    # Base case
    if n == 0:
        return 0
    elif n == 1:
        return 1

    # Recursive case
    else:
        return fibonacci_recursive(n-1) + fibonacci_recursive(n-2)
```

Python   >>>

```
>>> fibonacci_recursive(5)
Calculating F(5), Calculating F(4), Calculating F(3), Calculating F(2), Calculating F(1
Calculating F(0), Calculating F(1), Calculating F(2), Calculating F(1), Calculating F(0
Calculating F(3), Calculating F(2), Calculating F(1), Calculating F(0), Calculating F(1

5
```

$$F_n = F_{n-1} + F_{n-2}$$

Memoization in Python

Memoization is a concept coined in 1968 by Donald Michie from the Latin phrase memorandum (recall). Memoization is a software engineering tool used to accelerate equations by preserving (recollecting) previous equations. If repetitive function calls are made with much the same parameters, the prior values will be stored rather than redundant functions being replicated. We must use Memoization in this section to locate terms in the series of Fibonacci.

As a reference, the Fibonacci series is described to be the number of a total of two numbers.

```
def fibonacci(input_value):
    if input_value == 1:
        return 1
    elif input_value == 2:
        return 1
    elif input_value > 2:
        return fibonacci(input_value -1) + fibonacci(input_value -2)
```

Below are the simple examples that state if the amount of the input is equal to 1 or 2, returning 1. If the source input is higher than 2, enable recursive calls with the two previous amounts of Fibonacci.

Let us just display the very first 10 points now:

```
for i in range(1, 11):
    print("fib({}) = ".format(i), fibonacci(i))
```

```
fib(1)  =  1
fib(2)  =  1
fib(3)  =  2
fib(4)  =  3
fib(5)  =  5
fib(6)  =  8
fib(7)  =  13
fib(8)  =  21
fib(9)  =  34
fib(10) =  55
```

All appears to be okay. Let's really aim to demonstrate the very first 200 phrases:

```
for i in range(1, 201):
    print("fib({}) = ".format(i), fibonacci(i))
```

```
fib(20) =  6765
fib(21) =  10946
fib(22) =  17711
fib(23) =  28657
fib(24) =  46368
fib(25) =  75025
fib(26) =  121393
fib(27) =  196418
fib(28) =  317811
fib(29) =  514229
fib(30) =  832040
fib(31) =  1346269
fib(32) =  2178309
fib(33) =  3524578
fib(34) =  5702887
fib(35) =  9227465
fib(36) =  14930352
```

Let's really take the necessary actions to introduce the Memoization process. Let's create a dictionary to proceed:

```
fibonacci_cache = {}
```

First, our Memoization feature will be specified. Next, we test if the entry is in the dictionary that is the dictionary key. If the key is available, we retrieve the input/output worth:

```
def fibonacci_memo(input_value):
    if input_value in fibonacci_cache:
        return fibonacci_cache[input_value]
```

Next, we describe the base situations that suit the very first two possible values. If the sum of the inputs is 1 or 2, the output is set to 1:

```
def fibonacci_memo(input_value):
    ...

    if input_value == 1:
        value = 1
    elif input_value == 2:
        value = 1
```

First, we take the recursive situations into account. When the input is higher than 2, we determine the amount equivalent to the total of the two preceding contexts:

```
def fibonacci_memo(input_value):
    ...
    elif input_value > 2:
        value = fibonacci_memo(input_value -1) +
fibonacci_memo(input_value -2)
```

At the conclusion, we save the context and returns the results in our dictionary:

```
def fibonacci_memo(input_value):
    ...
    fibonacci_cache[input_value] = value
    return value
```

The entire function is:

```
def fibonacci_memo(input_value):
    if input_value in fibonacci_cache:
        return fibonacci_cache[input_value]
    if input_value == 1:
        value = 1
    elif input_value == 2:
        value = 1
    elif input_value > 2:
        value = fibonacci_memo(input_value -1) +
fibonacci_memo(input_value -2)
    fibonacci_cache[input_value] = value
    return value
```

Namespaces in Python

A namespace is a set of symbolic names traditionally understood and details about the entity referred by every initial. You should consider a namespace as a lexicon where the keys are entity initials, and the values themselves are the artifacts. Almost every pair of key values charts a title towards its entity.

Namespaces are not just awesome, as Tim Peters says. It's fun to squeal, and Python does it pretty thoroughly. There will be four kinds of namespaces in a python script:

- Assembled-in

- Local

- Containment

- Global

These have different lives. Just like Python runs a package, it generates and erases namespaces once they're no longer required. Usually, there will be several namespaces at any particular time.

The Terms Built-in

The built-in namespace includes all of the built-in artifacts in Python. These are always obtainable as Python starts running. With the following command you may list the items in the constructed-in namespace:

```
>>> dir(__builtins__)
['ArithmeticError', 'AssertionError', 'AttributeError',
 'BaseException','BlockingIOError', 'BrokenPipeError', 'BufferError',
 'BytesWarning', 'ChildProcessError', 'ConnectionAbortedError',
 'ConnectionError', 'ConnectionRefusedError', 'ConnectionResetError',
 'DeprecationWarning', 'EOFError', 'Ellipsis', 'EnvironmentError',
 'Exception', 'False', 'FileExistsError', 'FileNotFoundError',
 'FloatingPointError', 'FutureWarning', 'GeneratorExit', 'IOError',
 'ImportError', 'ImportWarning', 'IndentationError', 'IndexError',
 'InterruptedError', 'IsADirectoryError', 'KeyError', 'KeyboardInterrupt',
 'LookupError', 'MemoryError', 'ModuleNotFoundError', 'NameError', 'None',
 'NotADirectoryError', 'NotImplemented', 'NotImplementedError', 'OSError',
 'OverflowError', 'PendingDeprecationWarning', 'PermissionError',
 'ProcessLookupError', 'RecursionError', 'ReferenceError', 'ResourceWarning',
 'RuntimeError', 'RuntimeWarning', 'StopAsyncIteration', 'StopIteration',
 'SyntaxError', 'SyntaxWarning', 'SystemError', 'SystemExit', 'TabError',
 'TimeoutError', 'True', 'TypeError', 'UnboundLocalError',
 'UnicodeDecodeError', 'UnicodeEncodeError', 'UnicodeError',
 'UnicodeTranslateError', 'UnicodeWarning', 'UserWarning', 'ValueError',
 'Warning', 'ZeroDivisionError', '_', '__build_class__', '__debug__',
 '__doc__', '__import__', '__loader__', '__name__', '__package__',
 '__spec__', 'abs', 'all', 'any', 'ascii', 'bin', 'bool', 'bytearray',
 'bytes', 'callable', 'chr', 'classmethod', 'compile', 'complex',
 'copyright', 'credits', 'delattr', 'dict', 'dir', 'divmod', 'enumerate',
 'eval', 'exec', 'exit', 'filter', 'float', 'format', 'frozenset',
 'getattr', 'globals', 'hasattr', 'hash', 'help', 'hex', 'id', 'input',
 'int', 'isinstance', 'issubclass', 'iter', 'len', 'license', 'list',
 'locals', 'map', 'max', 'memoryview', 'min', 'next', 'object', 'oct',
 'open', 'ord', 'pow', 'print', 'property', 'quit', 'range', 'repr',
 'reversed', 'round', 'set', 'setattr', 'slice', 'sorted', 'staticmethod',
 'str', 'sum', 'super', 'tuple', 'type', 'vars', 'zip']
```

117

The Global Namespace

The global namespace includes all initials specified at the stage of the main script. Python generates the global namespace whenever the program code brain begins, and it persists in operation until the translator closes.

The translator also creates a global namespace for any subsystem, which the software helps with the import statement.

Local Namespace

This namespace contains a regular expression of local names. A namespace is provided by Python for each function named in a script. It keeps working until the function comes back.

Scope of Python objects

Scope refers to the coding region that is available from a single Python item. Therefore, from somewhere in the script, you cannot reach any single entity; the accessibility must be permitted by the context of the object. Let us take the example to grasp in-depth the very same:

```python
# Python program showing
# a scope of object

def some_func():
    print("Inside some_func")
    def some_inner_func():
        var = 10
        print("Inside inner function, value of var:",var)
    some_inner_func()
    print("Try printing var from outer function: ",var)
some_func()
```

Output:

```
Inside some_func
Inside inner function, value of var: 10

Traceback (most recent call last):
  File "/home/1eb47bb3eac2fa36d6bfe5d349dfcb84.py", line 8, in
    some_func()
  File "/home/1eb47bb3eac2fa36d6bfe5d349dfcb84.py", line 7, in some_func
    print("Try printing var from outer function: ",var)
NameError: name 'var' is not defined
```

Deep vs. Shallow Copy of Python Objects

Assignment statements in Python may not build object clones; they attach only object names. It generally might not create a change with immutable things.

But you could be looking for some way to make "real clones" or "copycats" of such objects for practice with declarative artifacts or sets of declarative items. Basically, you also want backups that you can alter while changing the actual concurrently. We will give you a description of how to duplicate or "copy" artifacts in Python 3 and even some of the notifications included in this post.

When it comes to copying objects, there is no variation between python 2 and 3. We should find them out in the document where there are variations.

Let us continue with how to copy the built-in collections of Python. Pythons implemented mutable objects such as lists, discs, and sets can be transferred to an existing collection by naming their factory functions:

```Python
new_list = list(original_list)
new_dict = dict(original_dict)
new_set = set(original_set)
```

This approach, nevertheless, does not work for custom objects and could only render shallow copies. There seems to be an interesting point amongst shallow and deep duplication for composite items including lists, dict, and sets:

- A shallow copy is a new set object, instead of a relation to the child items contained in the first. A shallow copy is effectively only one step profound. The duplication phase doesn't really resurface and will not produce clones of the child's objects.

- The copying cycle is repeated by a deep copy. This involves first creating a new set object and then complementing this iteratively with clones of the child's objects found in the initial. That ensures the entire entity tree moves to construct an individual replica of the object surface and all of its children.

How to Make Shallow Copy

For the given description we must make a new nesting list and then copy it using the factory function list ():

```
>>> xs = [[1, 2, 3], [4, 5, 6], [7, 8, 9]]
>>> ys = list(xs)   # Make a shallow copy
```

Ys also retains links to initial objects contained in xs since we created only a shallow copy of the actual set. Such children have not been copied. We have just been referenced in the replicated list afterward.

The adjustment would also represent the change in ys whenever you change one of the child items in xs since the two lists contain the very same child artifacts. The copy is a shallow, deep one-level version:

```Python
>>> xs[1][0] = 'X'
>>> xs
[[1, 2, 3], ['X', 5, 6], [7, 8, 9], ['new sublist']]
>>> ys
[[1, 2, 3], ['X', 5, 6], [7, 8, 9]]
```

How to Make Deep Copies?

Let us revisit the earlier case of list replication, albeit with one major change. In this turn, we will construct a deep copy that uses the copy framework deepcopy () function:

```
>>> import copy
>>> xs = [[1, 2, 3], [4, 5, 6], [7, 8, 9]]
>>> zs = copy.deepcopy(xs)
```

Nevertheless, if you render an adjustment to one of the child artifacts (xs), the deep copy (zs) will not be influenced by this alteration.

```
>>> xs[1][0] = 'X'
>>> xs
[[1, 2, 3], ['X', 5, 6], [7, 8, 9]]
>>> zs
[[1, 2, 3], [4, 5, 6], [7, 8, 9]]
```

All the initial and the replica artifacts are periods completely different. xs has been recurrently copied, along with all its artifacts for children:

The thing to keep in Mind

- Having an object shallow does not replicate child objects. The copy is, therefore, not entirely different from the source.

- A deep copy of an item recurrently copies objects for children. The replica is completely separate from the source, although it is sluggish to build a deep duplicate.

- You could copy random objects with the copy feature (such as customizable classes).

DECISION MAKING AND FLOW CONTROL

Decision Making

Decision making structures are required whenever you want a program to implement a course of action each time a test condition is satisfied.

A decision-making block starts with a Boolean expression. The program will proceed depending on whether the response is True or False.

Python supports the following decision-making structures

if statements

if else statements

if...elif...else statements

if statements

syntax:

if expression:

   statement(s)

Example:

```
age = int(input("Enter your age: "))
if age >= 18:
    print("Welcome to Wise Adults Forum!")
print("We accept members from age 18 and above.")
```

When a user responds with '19' to the prompt string, here's the onscreen output:

Enter your age: 19

Welcome to Wise Adults Forum!

We accept members from age 18 and above.

When a user's responds with '12':

Enter your age: 12

We accept members from age 18 and above.

if...else statements

In an if...else structure, Python executes the 'if block' if the test condition yields True and the 'else block' if the condition is False.

syntax:

if test condition:
   statement(s)

else: statement(s)

Example:

#this program checks if a food order is available
items = ['French Fries', 'Nuggets', 'Pizza', 'Pho', 'Ramen']

order = input("Please enter an order: ")
if order in items:
   print("You order of " + order + " will be served in 5 minutes.")
else:
   print("Sorry, " + order + " is not available at this time.")
If the user responds with 'Pizza', the output would be:

Please enter an order: Pizza
Your order of Pizza will be served in 5 minutes.
If the user enters 'Burger'

Please enter an order: Burger

Sorry, Burger is not available at this time.

if...elif...if statements

An if...elif...if structure facilitates the evaluation of multiple expressions. If the 'if test expression' is True, it executes the 'if block.' If False, it evaluates the elif (else if) block. If the 'elif text condition' is True, it executes the elif block. If False, it executes the else block.

syntax:

if test condition:
   if block
elif test condition:
   elif block
else:
   else block

Example:

#this program checks if an order is available

#if not available, it will check if the ordered item is on the pending list and prints an appropriate remark

#if the order is neither available nor pending, the program prints an appropriate remark

```python
available = ['French Fries', 'Nuggets', 'Pizza', 'Pho', 'Ramen']
pending = ['Barbeque', 'Cheeseburger', 'Tacos']

order = input("Please enter an order: ")
if order in available:
    print("You order of " + order + " will be served in 5 minutes.")
elif order in pending:
    print("Your order of " + order + " will be served in 15 minutes.")
else:
    print("Sorry, " + order + " is not available at this time.")
```

If the user enters Ramen, an item on the available list:

Please enter an order: Ramen
Your order of Ramen will be served in 5 minutes.

If the user enters 'Tacos', an item on the pending list
Please enter an order: Tacos
Your order of Tacos will be served in 15 minutes.
If the user enters Noodles which is not on the available or pending list:

Please enter an order: Noodles

Sorry, Noodles is not available at this time.

Flow Control

A loop is a program control structure that facilitates complicated execution paths and repetitive execution of a statement or block of statements.

For Loop

A 'for loop' is used to iterate over elements of ordered data types such as lists, tuples, or strings.

Syntax:

for val in sequence:

   statement(s)

In a 'for loop, the variable holds the value of each item on the sequence with every iteration. The loop runs until all items are processed.

Examples

For Loop over a string:

```
for letter in 'Finance':
    print('<**', letter, '**>')
```

If you run the loop, this would be the output:

```
<** F **>
<** i **>
<** n **>
<** a **>
<** n **>
<** c **>
<** e **>
```

For loop over a list:

```
#iterate over a list
animals = ['dog', 'cheetah', 'leopard', 'kangaroo', 'leopard']

For x in animals:
```

```
    print('A ' + x + ' is a cool animal')
print('These animals are great!'
```

If you run the loop, this will be your output:

A dog is a cool animal

A cheetah is a cool animal

A leopard is a cool animal

A kangaroo is a cool animal

A leopard is a cool animal

These animals are great!

Notice that after all the animal names in the list have been processed by the loop, control passes to the unindented print statement.

The While Loop

The 'while loop' is used when you want to repeatedly execute a statement or group of statements while the test condition is True. When it's no longer True, control passes to the line after the loop

syntax

```
while condition
    statement(s)
```

Example:

```
#program adds number up to an entered number
#total = 1+2+3...+number

x = int(input("Enter a number: "))
#initialize sum and counter
total = 0
ctr = 1
while ctr <= x:
    total = total + ctr
    ctr = ctr + 1
#print the sum
print("The sum is: ", total)
```

If you run the program and enter 1, 6, and 10, you will get these results

```
Enter a number: 1
The sum is:  1
Enter a number: 6
The sum is:  21        #1+2+3+4+5+6

Enter a number: 10        #1+2+3+4+5+6+7+8+9+10
The sum is:  55
```

Break Statement

A break statement ends the loop and passes control to the statement immediately after the loop. It allows the termination of the current iteration or the loop regardless of the test condition and effectively prevents the execution of the 'else' statement. It is used when an external condition requires immediate exit from the loop.

Example:

```
#loop ends once it reaches a given number
contestants = [1, 2, 3, 4, 5, 6, 7, 8, 9
for num in contestants:
  if num == 5:
    break
  print('In :', num)
print("Congratulations!")
```

Once it reaches number 5, the loop ends and control passes to the next unindented line:

In : 1

In : 2

In : 3

In : 4

Congratulations!

Continue Statement

The continue statement directs the program to proceed to the next iteration after reaching a specified item in the list.

To illustrate, you can use the above example and replace the break statement with the continue statement:

```
contestants = [1, 2, 3, 4, 5, 6, 7, 8, 9]
for num in contestants:
  if num == 5:
    continue
  print('In :', num)
print("Congratulations!")
```

When you run the program, it skips iteration for number 5 and proceeds to the other numbers on the list:

In : 1

In : 2

In : 3

In : 4

In : 6

In : 7

In : 8

In : 9

Congratulations!

Pass Statement

Pass is a null operation in which the interpreter reads the statement but does nothing. It is typically used as a place holder for a statement required by syntax but is not available when a program has to be run. Programmers use the pass statement in place of unwritten codes to allow them to test other parts of the program.

Syntax:

```
pass
```

Example:

#pass statement in an empty function block

```
def adder(a):
    pass
```

Try and Except Statements

Python's built-in exceptions cause a program to return an error whenever a problem occurs. When an error or exception occurs, the current process terminates and control passes to the calling process and so on until it is handled. Failure to handle the error or exception will cause the program to crash.

Try and except statements are used to handle program errors in Python. A critical area of a program is placed within the 'try clause' while the statement/s that will handle the exception is given within the 'except clause'.

Example:

```
try:
    x = int(input("Please enter a number: "))
    print("You entered %d." % x)
except ValueError:
    print("You entered an invalid character. Please try again.")
```

Python will attempt to execute the statement/s within the 'try block.' In this part of the program, there is a possibility that a value other than a number will be entered by a user. Hence, this block was placed under the try clause. Whenever a ValueError is encountered, control passes to the 'except block' which handles the error.

If you test the program using an integer and a letter input, here's what you would get:

Please enter a number: 5

You entered 5.

Please enter a number: You entered an invalid character. Please try again.

Exercise

✔ Password Verification ✔

You are given the following details from a company's database:

Users	Password
Marie	201624
Mark	MARKbest
Mandy	Man5254
Fred	9595

Instructions:

Prepare a program that will ask for the user's name. If the user's name does not match any of the names in the database, print 'Sorry, you don't have access to this system.' If the user's name matches one of the user names in the above database, ask the user to enter a password. If the given password matches the password under the user's name, print 'Thank you.' If the given password doesn't match the user's password, print 'You entered an invalid password.'

INPUT AND OUTPUT

So far, we've only been writing programs that only use data we have explicitly defined in the script. However, your programs can also take in input from the user and utilize it. Python lets us solicit inputs from the user with a very intuitively named function—the input () function. Writing out the code input () enables us to prompt the user for information, which we can further manipulate. We can take the user input and save it as a variable, print it straight to the terminal, or do anything else we might like.

When we use the input function, we can pass in a string. The user will see this string as a prompt, and their response to the prompt will be saved as the input value. For instance, if we wanted to query the user for their favorite food, we could write the following:

favorite_food = input ("What is your favorite food? ")

If you ran this code example, you would be prompted for your favorite food. You could save multiple variables this way and print them all at once using the print () function along with print formatting, as we covered earlier. To be clear, the text that you write in the input function is what the user will see as a prompt; it isn't what you are inputting into the system as a value.

When you run the code above, you'll be prompted for input. After you type in some text and hit the return key, the text you wrote will be stored as the variable favorite_food. The input command can be used along with string formatting to inject variable values into the text that the user will see. For instance, if we had a variable called user_name that stored the name of the user, we could structure the input statement like this:

favorite_food = input (" What is ()'s favorite food? "). format (" user name here")

Printing and Formatting Outputs

We've already dealt with the print () function quite a bit, but let's take some time to address it again here and learn a bit more about some of the more advanced things you can do with it.

By now, you've gathered that it prints whatever is in the parentheses to the terminal. Besides, you've learned that you can format the printing of statements with either the modulus operator (%) or the format function (. format ()). However, what should we do if we are in the process of printing a very long message?

In order to prevent a long string from running across the screen, we can use triple quotes that surround our string. Printing with triple quotes allows us to separate our print statements onto multiple lines. For example, we could print like this:

- print (''' By using triple quotes we can
- divide our print statement into multiple
- lines, making it easier to read. ''')

Formatting the print statement like that will give us:

- By using triple quotes, we can
- divide our print statement into multiple
- lines, making it easier to read.

What if we need to print characters that are equivalent to string formatting instructions? For example, if we ever needed to print out the characters "%s "or "%d, "we would run into trouble. If you recall, these are string formatting commands, and if we try to print these out, the interpreter will interpret them as formatting commands.

Here's a practical example. As mentioned, typing "/t" in our string will put a tab in the middle of our string. Assume we type the following:

- print ("We want a \t here, not a tab.")
- We'd get back this:
- We want a here, not a tab.

By using an escape character, we can tell Python to include the characters that come next as part of the string's value. The escape character we want to use is the "raw string" character, an "r" before the first quote in a string, like this:

- print (r"We want a \t here, not a tab.")
- So, if we used the raw string, we'd get the format we want back:
- We want a \t here, not a tab.

The "raw string" formatter enables you to put any combination of characters you'd like within the string and have it to be considered part of the string's value.

However, what if we did want the tab in the middle of our string? In that case, using special formatting characters in our string is referred to as using "escape characters." "Escaping" a string is a method of reducing the ambiguity in how characters are interpreted. When we use an escape character, we escape the typical method that Python uses to interpret certain characters, and the characters we type are understood to be part of the string's value. The escape primarily used in Python is the backslash (\). The backslash prompts Python to listen for a unique character to follow that will translate to a specific string formatting command.

We already saw that using the "\t" escape character puts a tab in the middle of our string, but there are other escape characters we can use as well.

\n - Starts a new line

\\ - Prints a backslash itself

\" - Prints out a double quote instead of a double quote marking the end of a string

\' - Like above but prints out a single quote

Exercise

Let's do another exercise that applies what we've covered in this section. You should try to write a program that does the following:

• Prompts the user for answers to several different questions.

• Prints out the answers on different lines using a single print statement.

Give this a shot before you look below for an answer to this exercise prompt.

If you've given this a shot, your answer might look something like this:

```
favorite_food = input ("What's your favorite food? :")

favorite_animal = input ("What about your favorite animal? :")

favorite_movie = input ("What's the best movie? :")

print ("Favorite food is: " + favorite_food + "\n" +

"Favorite animal is: " + favorite_animal + "\n" +

"Favorite movies is: " + favorite_movie)
```

We've covered a lot of ground in the first quarter of this book. We'll begin covering some more complex topics and concepts. However, before we move on, let's be sure that we've got the basics down. You won't learn the new concepts unless you are familiar with what we've covered so far, so for that reason, let's do a quick review of what we've learned so far:

• Variables: Variables are representations of values. They contain the value and allow the value to be manipulated without having to write it out every time. Variables must contain only letters, numbers, or underscores. Besides, the first character in a variable cannot be a number, and the variable name must not be one of Python's reserved keywords.

- Operators: Operators are symbols, which are used to manipulate data. The assignment operator (=) is used to store values in variables. Other operators in Python include: the addition operator (+), the subtraction operator (-), the multiplication operator (*), the division operator (/), the floor division operator (//), the modulus operator (%), and the exponent operator (**). The mathematical operators can be combined with the assignment operator. (Ex. +=, -=, *=).

- Strings: Strings are text data, declared by wrapping text in single or double-quotes. There are two methods of formatting strings; with the modulus operator or the. format () command. The "s," "d," and "f" modifiers are used to specify the placement of strings, integers, and floats.

- Integers: Integers are whole numbers, numbers that possess no decimal points or fractions. Integers can be stored in variables simply by using the assignment operator.

- Floats: Floats are numbers that possess decimal parts. The method of creating a float in Python is the same as declaring an integer, just choose a name for the variable and then use the assignment operator.

- Type Casting: Type casting allows you to convert one data type to another if the conversion is feasible (non-numerical strings cannot be converted into integers or floats). You can use the following functions to convert data types: int (), float (), and str ().

• Lists: Lists are just collections of data, and they can be declared with brackets and commas separating the values within the brackets. Empty lists can also be created. List items can be accessed by specifying the position of the desired item. The append () function is used to add an item to a list, while the del command and remove () function can be used to remove items from a list.

• List Slicing: List slicing is a method of selecting values from a list. The item at the first index is included, but the item at the second index isn't. A third value, a stepper value, can also be used to slice the list, skipping through the array at a rate specified by the value. (Ex. - numbers [0:9:2])

• Tuples: Tuples are like lists, but they are immutable; unlike lists, their contents cannot be modified once they are created. When a list is created, parentheses are used instead of brackets.

• Dictionaries: Dictionaries stored data in key/value pairs. When a dictionary is declared, the data and the key that will point to the data must be specified, and the key-value pairs must be unique. The syntax for creating a key in Python is curly braces containing the key on the left side and the value on the right side, separated by a colon.

• Inputs: The input () function gets an input from the user. A string is passed into the parenthesis, which the user will see when they are prompted to enter a string or numerical value.

• Formatting Printing: Triple quotes allows us to separate our print statement onto multiple lines. Escape characters are used to specify that certain formatting characters, like "\n" and "\t," should be included in a string's value. Meanwhile, the "raw string" command, "r," can be used to include all the characters within the quotes.

LEARNING ABOUT FUNCTIONS

Understanding the Concept of Function

Take a moment or two here and engage your mind a little. Think about it and try to come up with some vague idea of what functions truly are.

Functions are either user-defined or pre-defined. In either case, their job is to organize codes within a recallable function name. There are tons of pre-defined functions available within Python. We have already been using some of these again and again.

We already have a decent idea about functions that are built-in and pre-defined. These include and are not limited to input(), print(), and so many more. However, let's now look at how to create our function.

Let's begin with a traditional approach and write a block of code that welcomes the user with a friendly greeting. We will store this as a function named "welcome_message" so that we can call on this function later on.

```python
def welcome_message():

    print("Hello and welcome")

    print("Hope you have a great time")
```

```
print("Begin")

welcome_message()

print("End")
```

Let's begin learning and see what is happening in the block of code above. Firstly, for us to create our function, we need to define it first. The 'def' is a keyword that Python will look at and immediately understand that you are about to 'define' a new function. Next, we will need to name the function. While you can always name the function as you please, it is highly recommended and encouraged that you use names that are easy to understand and have a descriptive name. If we were to name this function anything other than welcome_message, we may know what it is as we wrote it, but for any other programmer out there, they may not understand.

Whenever you create a function, you need to use parentheses. You do not have to pass any information through it so leave them as they are. Now, we need to add the colon mark.

What happens when you use a colon at the end of a statement? Your cursor gets indented in the following line. That means your cursor will be slightly far from the actual starting point. This is to denote to the programmer that he/she is about to type something that would hold value for a command or a statement above it. In this case, we are trying to define the function.

Let's then use two print commands and place our greeting messages. That is it! You have now created your very first function. You can now recall it as many times as you like. However, should you try to call on this function a line or two before the 'def' command, Python will have no idea what you're talking about. Why? That has everything to do with the fact that Python reads a program line by line. By the time it arrives on the line where you called a function, it would check with the previous lines and not find anything relatable as the actual 'def' step was carried out in a step following this.

After this, let's now use our function and see how it works. Remember, the function holds two printable messages for our users. For our reference, we will now create a 'begin' and an 'end' message. This would allow us and the programmer to know where the regular messages are and where the function lies. Use your function with empty parentheses between the two print commands as shown above. If you like, you can remove these print commands and just type in your function number to see the results.

A quick tip for all! If you come across the annoying wiggly lines, simply hover your mouse over it and you will find out what the expected or suggested solution is. In this case, if you remove the two-line spaces, you should see a suggestion saying this:

Whenever you define a function, you will always be required to leave at least two blank lines before proceeding on with the codes.

Using Various Functions

Python was created with simplicity in mind. It was also created to minimize the work and maximize the output. If you use the codes and the functions wisely, you will surely be making the most out of this programming language. It is also noticeable that most of the things you learn about Python and its functions, parameters, methods, and such will help you learn other languages quicker, so do pay attention.

Parameters

Our eagle-eyed readers may have noticed something about the function we just created a few minutes ago. Unlike most of the functions, we did not pass any information through the parentheses at all. Why that happens is something we will come to know about once we understand exactly what parameters are in Python.

Parameters are used as place-holders for receiving information. These are what we, as well as users, provide to the program in order for it to work more accurately. There are some cases and functions where arguments are not required for them to do their basic operation. However, if you provide an argument to these functions, they will provide you with a more specific output. Of course, it does depend on the availability of the said parameter. You cannot force a function to do something it is not designed to do.

Now, let's look at our function. It is certainly missing something. If you currently print the welcome_user function, it would say everything but will not contain the name of the user at all. Surely, it would look a lot nicer for us if we could somehow use this function to use the name of the user and add it to the greeting.

Luckily, we can do just that! For that, we first need to add the 'name' parameter in the first line, where we began defining our function. Simple type name between the parentheses and you will see the text turn grey. This confirms that the word has been added as a parameter. Now, we wish to print the name of this user along with the greetings we have defined within the function. For this example, let's assume that the user is named Fred.

def welcome_message(name):

```
print("Begin")

print("Hello and welcome {name}!")

print("Hope you have a great time")

print("End")

welcome_message('Fred')

Begin

Hello and welcome Fred!

Hope you have a great time

End
```

Finally! We have a name to add to our greetings. You can add another line of code by using our function and passing a different name now. See what happens then.

When we set a parameter for a function and then call upon the function without providing it with an argument or the bit of information that goes between the parentheses, it will provide us with an error, except for a few.

Now, let's make our function a little more dynamic and add another parameter. Let's add a parameter that allows the program to print out the last name of the user. Now, our code should look something like this:

```python
def welcome_message(name, last_name):

    print("Hello and welcome {name} {last_name}!")

    print("Hope you have a great time")


print("Begin")

welcome_message('Fred', 'William')

print("End")
```

The point to learn here, apart from being able to add parameters, is the fact that 'Fred' and 'William' are being used in a specific order. Should you type it the other way around, Python will print these as they are. This is because of their position concerning the defined parameters. The first value Python reads here, it will automatically link it with the first parameter. This can cause a little confusion, especially if the last name becomes the first name.

These arguments are called as positional arguments. To further show their importance, let's remove the last name from the argument above.

```python
print("Begin")

welcome_message('Fred')

print("End")
```

Traceback (most recent call last):

Begin

 File "C:/Users/Smith/PycharmProjects/MyFirstGo/PosArg.py", line 7, in <module>

  welcome_message('Fred')

TypeError: welcome_message() missing 1 required positional argument: 'last_name'

So, the system does not allow us to continue as we have removed an element. This time, type in the last name first followed by the first name and see if it makes any difference. When you run the program now, you should be able to see this:

```python
print("Begin")
```

```
welcome_message('Fred', 'William')

print("End")

Begin

Hello and welcome William Fred!

Hope you have a great time

End
```

Now, the sequence kind of work. The only issue is that it has gotten the name wrong. Now, the last name is being portrayed and printed as the first name. That is rather embarrassing, isn't it?

The above errors either state that we are missing one required positional argument or show that we placed the wrong name in the wrong place. Positional arguments are such arguments whose position matters a lot. If you miss out on the position altogether, you will end up with an error. If you type in something else, as we did in our last example, you will produce incorrect results. To correct it, simply provide the last name after the first name.

There is one more way you can have these dealt with by using what is termed as 'keyword arguments.' These are the kind of arguments whose position does not matter at all and Python will still continue to function properly regardless of their position in the parentheses. To pass a keyword argument, you will need to do the following:

print("Begin")

welcome_message(last_name='William', name='Fred')

print("End")

Begin

Hello and welcome Fred William!

Hope you have a great time End

Now that's more like it. Things are looking right at how we want them. Notice how, even though we wrote in the wrong order, Python picked up and sorted the order for us. That is because we made our entries or arguments into keyword arguments using the name= or last_name= parameter and combining it with arguments. This allows Python to draw information and understand which of these two comes first in order as defined originally in our function.

Factually speaking, you will not be using these quite a lot, but it is always an advantage to know the ways to overcome certain issues. Normally, you or any other programmer would be able to see the data and read it easily if you simply follow the rules and type the first name followed by the last name. Make the code as easy as you can for everyone to read and understand.

Exercise

Here is the updated version of a program we designed to check insurance prices a person would have to pay if he/she was above or below a certain age. Your objective is to convert this into a function. Your function should have three fields set to receive input from the user.

1. Name

2. Age

3. Actual insurance cost

Updated code:

Insurance = 1000

age = int(input('Your age: '))

is_old = age > 40

```python
is_young = age <= 28

has_license = input('Do you have a license? ')

if has_license.lower() == 'Yes':

    has_license = True

elif has_license.lower() != 'Yes':

    has_license = False

if is_old and has_license:

    Insurance = Insurance / 2

    print("Your insurance cost is ${Insurance}")

elif is_young and has_license:

    Insurance = Insurance // 1.50

    print("You will need to pay ${Insurance}")

else:

    print('You are not eligible for insurance at this time')
```

DICTIONARY

When the key is known dictionaries will retrieve values.

Creating a Dictionary

A dictionary is generated by having items in curly braces demarcated by a comma. A dictionary element has a key and a matching value. The key and value in Python are captured as a pair. Normally, key: value. Keys have to be immutable and unique.

Example:

Start IDLE.

Type the following:

dict_mine= {}   #Empty dictionary

 # dictionary with integer keys

dict_mine= {2: 'pawpaw', 4: 'rectangle'}   #dictionary with integer keys

dict_mine = {'student': 'Brenda',2:[12, 14, 13]}#dictionary with integer keys

162

dict_mine = dict({2:'student': 'Brenda' })

dict_mine = dict([(2, 'pawpaw'), (4, 'rectangle')])

Accessing Elements from a Dictionary

Dictionary uses keys instead of indexing to access values. The keys can be within the square brackets or with the get() method.

Example:

Start IDLE.

Navigate to the File menu and click New Window.

Type the following:

dict_mine = {'name':'James', 'age': 62}

print(dict_mine['name'])

print(dict_mine.get('age'))

Add or Modify Dictionary Elements

For dictionaries, they are mutable implying that we can modify the value of current items using the assignment operator. The value will get updated if the key is already existing else we will have to add a new key: the dictionary value couple.

Start IDLE.

Navigate to the File menu and click New Window.

Type the following:

dict_mine={'student':'James','age':62}

dict_mine['age'] = 37

print(dict_mine)

dict_mine['address'] = 'New York'

print(dict_mine)

Removing/Deleting Elements from a Dictionary

Example:

Start IDLE.

Navigate to the File menu and click New Window.

Type the following:

my_squares={10:100,8:64,12:224}

```
print(my_squares.pop(2))

print(my_squares)

print(my_squares.popitem())

print(my_squares)

del my_squares[4]

print(my_squares)

my_squares.clear()

print(squares)

del my_squares
```

Dictionary Methods in Python

Example:

Start IDLE.

Navigate to the File menu and click New Window.

Type the following:

```
scores ={}.fromkeys(['Chemistry','Spanish','Pyschology'], 0)

print(scores)
```

```
for item in marks.items():

    print(item)
```

Start IDLE.

Navigate to the File menu and click New Window

Type the following:

```
list(sorted(scores.keys()))
```

Dictionary Comprehension in Python

```
my_squares = {y: y*y for y in range(5)}

print(my_squares)
```

Alternatively, the program can be written as:

```
my_power = {}

for y in range(5):

    power[y] = y*y
```

Odd Items Only Dictionary

Example:

Start IDLE.

Navigate to the File menu and click New Window.

Type the following:

squares_odd={y:y*y for y in range(10) if y%2==1}

print(squares_odd)

Membership Test in a Dictionary

Using the keyword in, we can evaluate if a key is in a particular dictionary. The membership tests should be used for dictionary keys and not for dictionary values.

Example:

Start IDLE.

Navigate to the File menu and click New Window.

Type the following:

my_squares = {10: 100, 6: 36, 8: 64, 11: 121}

print(11 in my_squares)

print(36 in squares)

Practice Exercise

Given:

square_dict={2:4,6:36,8:64}

Use membership to test if 6 exist in the dictionary.

Use membership, test if 36 exist in the dictionary.

Iteration in a Dictionary

We use the for loop to iterate through each key in a particular dictionary.

Inbuilt Functions

Example:

Start IDLE.

Navigate to the File menu and click New Window.

Type the following:

your_squares = {2: 4, 4: 16, 6: 36, 8: 64, 10: 100}

print(len(your_squares))

print(sorted(your_squares))

for i in squares:

   print(your_squares[i])

Exercise

Give the following set, setm=set(["Blue","Yellow"])

Write a working program to copy the set elements.

Display the new set.

Clear the set.

Print the latest status of the set.

Given the setr=set(["Knock","Up"])

Write a simple program to copy the set elements.

Write a working program to display the latest status of the set.

Write a simple program clears the elements of the set.

Display the latest status of the set.

Delete the entire set using del.

Given m=frozenset([11,12,13,14,15]) and n=([13,14,15,16,17])

Use the isdisjoint() to test if the sets have no shared elements.

Write a program to return a new set with items in the set that are not in the others.

Write a union of sets m and n.

Write an intersection of sets n and m.

Write a program to pop an item in set n.

Write a program that appends element 21 to the set m.

Check to see if set m has element 14 using a built-in keyword.

Use discard() to drop all items in the set m.

Given this set second_set = {"berry", "pineaple", "melon"}

Write a Python program to update the set with these elements at a go "mango," "guava," "plum"

Find the length of this set using the len().

Use remove() to clear the set.

Given {(, 17, 19, 21)

Use set constructor set() to construct a set named third_set in Python.

Use the add() method to add "Kim" to the set.

Pop an element from the set using pop().

Update the set using update() to include {43,41,40}

Given setq=([13,2,17,8,19])

Find the minimum value in the set using inbuilt features of Python.

Find the maximum value in the set using inbuilt features of Python.

Given setb=([5,"K", 8, 1])

Use the for a statement to write a Python program that iterates through the set elements.

Given

diction1={11:12,12:27}

diction2={13:52,13:57}

Create a python program to concatenate the dictionaries in one.

USING FILES

We'll now look at how we can work with external files.

We've seen how to we can get input from the user using input(). But, sometimes, if we need to work with a lot of data, it's more common to use files instead of manual inputs.

This chapter will teach you how!

Reading Files

In this first example, we are going to read from a plain text file. Let's start: create a file with the following text.

Learn Python and Learn It Well

Save this file as myfile.txt in your desktop. Then, open IDLE and write the code below. Save this file as fileOperation.py, again on your desktop.

```
f = open ('myfile.txt', 'r')

firstline = f.readline()

secondline = f.readline()

print (firstline)
```

print (secondline) f.close()

The first line has a specific function: open the file.

Before reading from any file, we must open it. The open() function does exactly that.

The 1st parameter is simply the file path.

In case you didn't keep fileOperation.py and myfile.txt in the same directory, you'll need to add, before 'myfile.txt', the full path where you stored the text file. For example, if you saved it in a folder named 'PythonFiles' in your C drive, you need to code 'C:\\PythonFiles\\myfile.txt.'

The other parameter is the file open mode. Commonly used modes are:

- 'r' mode: For reading only.
- 'w' mode: For writing only.

If the desired file doesn't exist, it'll be now created.

If the specified file already exists, existing data on the file will be erased and you'll start with a plain one.

- 'a' mode: To append.

If the desired file doesn't exist, it'll be now created.

If the specified file already exists, existing data on the file will be kept and you'll start writing at the bottom of the file.

- 'r+' mode: For reading and writing.

After you open the file, the following code

- firstline = f.readline() Is useful to read the first line in the file and assign it to the variable.

Every time the readline() function is called, it reads a new line from the file.

In our program, readline() was called two times. So the first two lines will be read.

You'll find that a line break is inserted after every line you write in the file.

This is caused by the readline() function: it automatically adds the '\n' characters to the end of each line. In case you don't want that double line between each line of text, you can execute

- print (firstline, end = ''). This will remove the new line characters for the following output.

After reading and printing the two lines, the last line, f.close(), simply closes the file.

You should always close the file once you're done accessing it, so the system can free up some system resources.

Read files with a loop

The readline() function we described above to read a text file, is not enough to read a file with an undefined row number.

The solution is a loop: here's how you can do that.

f = open ("myfile.txt",'r')

for line in f:

 print (line, end = '')

f.close()

As you can guess, the loop cycles through the text file, line by line.

Writing to a File

Now that we've discovered how to open and read a file, let's move on and start writing into it.

To do so, we'll use the append mode, identified with 'a.'

It's also possible to use the 'w' mode that will erase and replace all the content of the file.

f = open ('myfile.txt', 'a')

f.write('\nAny new row will be appended.')

f.write('\nHere is it!')

f.close()

Now we use the write() function to append the two sentences to the file, each starting on a new line entirely because we used the escape characters '\n.'

Exercise 1

In the program that we've coded so far, I've avoided using the division operator. Can you modify the program so that it will create questions with the division sign too? How would you check the user's answer against the correct answer?

Hint: Check out the round() function.

Exercise 2

Sometimes, the question generated may result in an answer that is very large or very small. For example, question 6*[8^9/1]^3 will give the answer 14507109853755550096474112.

It is very uncomfortable for users to calculate and put in such a large number. Hence, we want to avoid answers that are too big or small. Can you edit the program to prevent questions that brings out answers greater than 50 000 or smaller than -50000?

Exercise 3

The last challenge exercise is the most difficult. So far, brackets are missing in the questions generated. Can you modify the program so that the questions use brackets too? An example of a question will be 2 + (3*7 -1) + 5.

Have fun with these exercises.

TESTING YOUR CODE

When creating a program, you do not just write code. You have to test it.

At this point, your only methods of testing your code are to run the script, wait for errors (if any) and test it using the interpreter.

Be that as it may, there is another method to test your code. And that is by using the unit test module. Inside the module, there are multiple functions you can use to test your code.

By the way, you may ask - why the need for a "unittest" if you can test your code by running it or checking it one by one inside the interpreter?

First, using a unit test is ideal for messy code. If other people cannot read your code, then unit test to see things that might go wrong. A unit test is much easier than manually testing one line of spaghetti code.

Second, a unit test is much faster to do. It is easy to test using the interpreter and running the script, but if you have hundreds of statements, a unit test is the best way to go.

Testing a function

It is advisable to perform the unit test when the code is nearly finished. The biggest problem with unit testing is that it can waste time when performed at the wrong time repeatedly. This is debatable, however.

Anyway, create a unit test in a module. You can do it with an interpreter, but it can be inconvenient since running the test will automatically close the window.

The first step in creating a unit test code is to import the unittest framework. Then you need to define a unit test subclass with TestCase from unittest.

For example:

import unittest

class Test1(unittest.TestCase):

To perform the testing, you need to create methods for the cases that you want to test.

Note that most methods that you will inherit from the TestCase super class are assert methods (e.g., assertEqual(), assertNotEqual(), assertIs(), etcetera). These methods often have two parameters with assertTrue(), assertFalse(), assertIsNone(), and assertIsNotNone() having one parameter only.

These two parameters of most assert methods are tested according to the assert method used.

For example, assertEqual() checks if parameter a is equal to parameter b. If it is equal, it will return a passing mark. If it is not, it will return a failing mark. For example:

```
import unittest

class Test(unittest.TestCase):

    def test1(self):

        self.assertEqual(1, 1)

unittest.main()
```

To run the test, you must execute the main() callable of the unittest framework. Once executed, it will execute all the tests that you created. After that, it will print information about the test on the console. This information includes an error, score, and time consumed.

To have a little bit control in the test execution, add an input() function in the beginning of the script. For example:

```
import unittest

input("Press enter to start the test.")

class Test(unittest.TestCase):
```

180

```python
    def test1(self):

        self.assertEqual(1, 1)

unittest.main()
```

If you run this test, it will display this information.

Press enter to start the test.

.

Ran 1 test in 0.000s

OK

The information tells the developer that it ran the single test method in the script and it took less than 0.0001 seconds to finish it. Since it immediately displayed the test result and OK line, that means it found no error.

The test1() method passed since 1 is equal to 1.

Here is an example that will result to an error:

```python
import unittest

input("Press enter to start the test.")

class Test(unittest.TestCase):
```

```python
    def test1(self):

        self.assertEqual(1, 0)

unittest.main()
```

Press enter to start the test.

F

==

FAIL: test1 (__main__.test)

Traceback (most recent call last):

  File "C:\P37\test.py", line 6, in test1

    self.assertEqual(1, 0)

AssertionError: 1 != 0

Ran 1 test in 0.000s

FAILED (failures=1)

The method to use when testing a function depends on the purpose of a function. But generally, all you need to do is to include one of the methods inside your TestCase's class. For example:

```python
import unittest

input("Press enter to start the test.")

def onlyReturn1():
    return 1

def onlyReturn2():
    return "2"

class Test(unittest.TestCase):
    def test1(self):
        self.assertIsInstance(onlyReturn1(), int)

        self.assertIsInstance(onlyReturn2(), int)

unittest.main()
```

Press enter to start the test.

F

==

=========================

FAIL: test1 (__main__.test)

183

Traceback (most recent call last):

  File "C:\P37\test.py", line 11 in test1

   self.assertIsInstance(onlyReturn2(), 0)

AssertionError: '2' is not an instance of <class 'int'>

Ran 1 test in 0.000s

FAILED (failures=1)

By checking the context of the program, it is expected that the functions onlyReturn1() and onlyReturn2() should only return int class objects. To check that, the example use assertIsInstance() method.

Since onlyReturn2() returns a string value ('2'), the test failed. You may have noticed that there was more than one assert method in the test method, but it only returned an error for one line and the result said it only ran 1 test.

One test method equates to one test. Also, when a test encounters a failure, it stops processing the rest of the method since it basically received an exception.

Exercise

Your practice exercise is to create at least ten test methods and check the programs you made. Remember that the practice exercise chapter that told you to create the eight programs you listed? Yes. Those are the programs that you should use your unit tests on.

If you have not created those programs yet, you should try and do so now. You are more than ready to program with Python, and surely, you can make a decent version of the programs you wanted.

CONDITIONAL AND ITERATIVE PROGRAMMING

Code indentation

Python uses indents. The concept of code indentation plays a major role in Python. Remember, we have not used indenting in any part of the code in previous examples. This is because if we do, the Python interpreter will think of it as a part of a code block which is a part of a condition, function, or loop (We will understand each of them shortly).

Your code must follow a consistent indentation such as four whitespaces or tabs. The amount of indentation is your choice, but you must use the same indents throughout that code block. If you try to indent any line of the code separately, the Python interpreter will throw an error message saying "unexpected indent" and the entire code will not work. If you want to execute a sequence of code, place the code right before the line starts. The indentation is only done in a block of code that is followed by a condition, function, or loop. Below is an example of writing Python code in the wrong way:

```
1    print("My")
2    print("Name")
3        print("Is")        # "Unexpected indent" error will occur here
4    print("Python")
```

Conditional statements

In the earlier examples, we have been programming in a sequential manner, which means that statements were being performed one after another and followed a sequential pattern. The conditional statements modify the sequential approach and are basically used to specify which block of code is to be executed first depending on some condition. These statements are supposed to return one of the Boolean values (true or false). They identify the current value of various variables used in code. These statements are called "conditional" because they work according to the current state of the program.

How it works

We have already studied comparison operators and their types in the Day 2 section. Comparison operators are a part of the conditional statement. If a conditional statement returns true then the block of code that is affiliated with it will be executed. If it returns false, then the entire block of code affiliated with it will be ignored by the Python interpreter.

Here is an example for a better understanding of how a conditional statement works. This is just a basic syntax of conditional statements.

```
1   Condition 1 (expression(s) 1 containing comparison operators)
2         print("hello")
3         print("from")
4         print("the code inside")
5         print("condition 1")
6
7   Condition 2 (expression(s) 2 containing comparison operators)
8         print("hello")
9         print("from")
10        print("the code inside")
11        print("condition 2")
```

Remember that similar code indentation is used after every condition to denote that it is a part of a similar code block.

The interpreter will check condition 1 because it comes first before condition 2. If condition 1 is met or simply expression 1 returns true then its block of code will be executed. Thus, the lines print ("hello"), print ("from"), print ("the code inside"), and print ("condition 1") will be executed. Then the interpreter will check condition 2, if the condition does not meet i.e. the expression 2 does not return true, then the lines print("hello") print("from"), print("the code inside"), and print("condition 2") will be completely ignored because they are in the block of condition 2.

Usage and working of if, elif, and else statements

The 'if' statement takes the result of the expression (a condition) and tells the interpreter to execute its block of code if the result of the expression is true. It is written in this way:

188

```
if <condition>:

Line 1

Line 2

...
```

However, the "if" statement is not bound to take an expression as a condition. You can directly pass Boolean values, numeric values, or strings to it as a condition.

Remember that for Numeric values, the empty values (0, 0.00, ...) will be considered as false, and all the values except empty values (even 0.00000000001) will be considered as true. For strings, the empty string ("") will be considered as false and all the strings except empty strings will have some value in programming languages so they will be considered as true.

The 'elif' statement also works exactly as if statement. The 'elif' statement does not work if there is no if statement placed before it. It consists of "else" and "if." The difference is that the 'elif' statement checks the condition only when the return type of if statement that is placed before it, is false.

Let's have a better understanding of it:

```
if <condition>:

line 1 inside if
```

line 2 inside *if*

elif <condition>

line 1 inside *elif*

line 2 inside *elif*

If the condition of 'if' statement is true, then the interpreter will execute both of the lines inside the 'if' statement and it will ignore the 'elif' statement because the first 'if' statement has been executed.

If the condition of the 'if' statement is false, then the interpreter will ignore the lines written in the 'if' block and jump to the 'elif' statement and see if the condition of the elif statement is met. If it is, then the block of 'elif' statement will be executed otherwise ignored (just like if statement). You can place as many 'elif' statements (one after another) like:

if <condition>:

// some code

// some code

elif <condition>: (1)

line 1

line 2

```
elif <condition>: (2)

line 1

line 2

elif <condition>: (3)

line 1

line 2

...

elif <condition>: (n)

line 1

line 2
```

Each 'elif' statement will only get the interpreter's attention when all of the conditional statements before it, return false. Let's say the first 'elif' gets true, then the interpreter will ignore all upcoming 'elif' statements.

The 'else' is a statement that also contains a block of code to be executed. However, the 'else' statement does not contain any condition. It is placed after 'elif' statement or 'if' statement if there is no 'elif' statement. Its block of code runs only when all the conditions placed before it is identified as false.

In other words, the code block of an else statement runs when none of the code blocks are executed before the else statement.

Let's have a better understanding of it:

if <condition>:

line 1

line 2

elif <coniditon>:

line 1

line 2

else:

line 1

line 2

If both the 'if' and 'elif' statements are false then regardless of any condition, the code block of the 'else' statement will be executed.

Code example

Enough of the theory! Let's consider a scenario where a variable of numeric type is checked whether it belongs to the range 1 – 10 or 11 – 20. If it belongs to one of the ranges, display the range as output. If it doesn't belong to any range, then show that it is out of range.

```
1    my_numeric_value = 21
2    range_1 = "1 - 10"
3    range_2 = "11 - 20"
4    if my_numeric_value >= 1 and my_numeric_value<=10:
5        print("The range is", range_1)
6    elif my_numeric_value >= 11 and my_numeric_value<=20:
7        print("The range is", range_2)
8    else:
9        print("It is out of range")
```

Exercises

1) Write a program that calculates the percentage based on total marks and marks obtained and checks:

a. If the percentage is above or equal to 90, display "A grade."

b. If the percentage is below 90 but above or equal to 80, display "B grade."

c. Else, display "F grade."

Consider total marks = 500 and marks obtained = 450.

2) Write a program that checks if the string has a value:

a. "Ball", display "Let's play ball."

b. "Basketball", display "I love Michael Jordan."

c. If it is not equal to any of the strings specified, display "I don't know it."

Consider the string "Volleyball" for comparing.

VARIABLES AND CONSTANTS IN PYTHON

Why Variables Are needed?

For any programming language, the basic part is to store the data in memory and process it. No matter what kind of operation we are going to perform, we must have the object of operation. It is difficult for a skillful woman to cook without rice. In Python language, constants and variables are the main ones. In fact, both of them are identification codes used by program designers to access data contents in memory.

The biggest difference between the two is that the contents of variables will change with the execution of the program, while the contents of constants are fixed forever. In the process of program execution, it is often necessary to store or use some data. For example, if you want to write a program to calculate the mid-term exam results, you must first input the students' results, and then output the total score, average score, and ranking after calculation. This chapter describes how to store and access this data.

Variable Naming and Assignment

In a program, program statements or instructions tell the computer which Data to access and execute step by step according to the instructions in the program statements. These data may be words or numbers. What we call variable is the most basic role in a programming language, that is, a named memory unit allocated by the compiler in programming to store changeable data contents.

The computer will store it in "memory" and take it out for use when necessary. In order to facilitate identification, it must be given a name. We call such an object "variable."

For example:

> > firstsample = 3

>>>second sample= 5

> > > result = firstsample+secondsample

In the above program statement, firstsample, secondsample, result are variables, and number 3 is the variable value of firstsample. Since the capacity of memory is limited, in order to avoid wasting memory space, each variable will allocate memory space of different sizes according to requirements, so "Data Type" is used to regulate it.

Variable declaration and assignment

Python is an object-oriented language, all data are regarded as objects, and the method of an Object reference is also used in variable processing. The type of variable is determined when the initial value is given, so there is no need to declare the data type in advance. The value of a variable is assigned with "=" and beginners easily confuse the function of the assignment operator (=) with the function of "equal" in mathematics. In programming languages, the "=" sign is mainly used for assignment.

The syntax for declaring a variable is as follows:

variable name = variable value

e.g.

number = 10.

The above expression indicates that the value 10 is assigned to the variable number. In short, in Python language, the data type does not need to be declared in advance when using a variable, which is different from that in C language, which must be declared in advance before using a variable. Python interpretation and operation system will automatically determine the data type of the variable according to the value of the variable given or set.

For example, the data type of the above variable number is an integer. If the content of the variable is a string, the data type of the variable is a string.

Constant

Constant refers to the value that the program cannot be changed during the whole execution process. For example, integer constants: 45, -36, 10005, 0, etc., or floating-point constants: 0.56, -0.003, 1.234E2, etc. Constants have fixed data types and values.

The biggest difference between variable and constant is that the content of the variable changes with the execution of the program, while the constant is fixed. Python's constant refers to the literal constant, which is the literal meaning of the constant. For example, 12 represents the integer 12. The literal constant is the value written directly into the Python program.

If literal constants are distinguished by data type, there will be different classifications, for example, 1234, 65, 963, and 0 are integer literal constants. The decimal value is the literal constant of the floating-point types, such as 3.14, 0.8467, and 744.084. As for the characters enclosed by single quotation marks (') or double quotation marks ("), they are all string literal constants. For example," Hello World "and" 0932545212 "are all string literal constants.

Formatting Input and Output Function

In the early stage of learning Python, the program execution results are usually output from the control panel, or the data input by the user is obtained from the console. Before, we often use the print () function to output the program's execution results. This section will look at how to call the print () function for print format and how to call the input () function to input data.

The print format

The print () function supports the print format. There are two formatting methods that can be used, one is the print format in the form of "%" and the other is the print format in the form function. "%" print format formatted text can use "%s" to represent a string, "%d" to represent an integer, and "%f" to represent a floating-point number.

The syntax is as follows:

PRINT (formatted text (parameter 1, parameter 2, ..., parameter n))

For example:

score = 66

Print ("History Score: %d"% score")

Output

Result: History Score: 66

%d is formatted, representing the output integer format.

The print format can be used to control the position of the printout so that the output data can be arranged in order.

For example:

print("%5s history result: %5.2f"% ("Ram,"95))

The output results of the sample program

print("%5s history results: %5.2f"% ("Raj,"80.2))

The formatted text in the above example has two parameters, so the parameters must be enclosed in brackets, where %5s indicates the position of 5 characters when outputting, and when the actual output is less than 5 characters, a space character will be added to the left of the string.

%5.2f represents a floating-point number with 5 digits output, and the decimal point occupies 2 digits. The following example program outputs the number 100 in floating-point number, octal number, hexadecimal number and binary number format using the print function, respectively.

You can practice with this example program:

[Example Procedure: print_%.py]

Integer Output

visual = 100 in Different Decimal Numbers

print ("floating point number of number %s: %5.1f"% (visual,visual)) print ("octal of number %s: %o"% (visual,visual))

print ("hex of number %s: %x"% (visual,visual))

The execution result of the print ("binary of number %s: %s"% (visual,bin(visual))) will be displayed.

Exercise

-The pocket money bookkeeping butler designed a Python program that can input the pocket money spent seven days a week and output the pocket money spent every day. The sample program illustrates that this program requires the user name to be entered, and then the sum of spending for each day of the week can be entered continuously, and the pocket money spent for each day can be output.

Program code shows that the following is the complete program code of this example program.

[example program: money.py]

pocket money bookkeeping assistant

```
# -*- coding: utf-8 -*-
```

"""

You can enter pocket money spent 7 days a week and output the pocket money spent every day.

```
"""

name = value ("Give name:")

working1 = value ("Give the total amount of pocket money for
the first working:")

working2 = value ("Give the total amount of pocket money for
the next working:")

working3 = value ("Give the total amount of pocket money for
the third working:")

working4 = value ("Give the total amount of pocket money for
the fourth working:")

working5 = value ("Give the total spending of pocket money for
the fifth working:")

working6 = value ("Give the total spending of pocket money for
the sixth working:")

working7 = input ("Give the total allowance for the seventh
working:")

print("{0:<8}{1:^5}{2:^5}{3:^5}{4:^5}{5:^5}{6:^5}{7:^5}." \

format("name,""working1,""working2,""working3," \
```

```
"working4,""working5,""working6," \

"working7"))

print("{0:<8}{1:^5}{2:^5}{3:^5}{4:^5}{5:^5}{6:^5}{7:^5}." \

format(name,working1,working2,working3,working4,working5,
working6,working7))

ave=total/7

print("total cost: {0:<8} average daily cost {1: 5}." format (total,
ave))
```

With this, we have completed a brief explanation regarding python and its basic concepts that are necessary for understanding traditional programming methodology. In the next chapter, we will discuss in detail about Operators and other moderate level topics that are necessary for a clear understanding of programming.

CONCLUSION

Sometimes, as a coder, it can be fun just making a program that looks nice. A lot of people fail to realize that quality is a large aspect of an algorithm. It can also be that people just don't have the skill set of a coder, so we haven't said to tell them how to write bad code yet.

There are also people who want to do things such as 'Hello, World!', through their code. This in itself is quite fun, but it's not particularly useful. For this reason, we're going to say that you should not do things like this. If you insist on writing this, then you might as well use a high-level programming language, or use a library to do it.

If you just wanted to write 'Hello, World!' then you should write a better 'Hello, World' in your own language. We do not want to hear how there is a 'Hello, World' or 'Fibonacci numbers' kata for every language. Unless you're writing something nice, there's no point in doing it

Instead, we're going to try something new. We're going to write in a way that will be useful in everyday programming. Python is a programming language that has a lot to offer, so we're going to try to re-purpose a lot of Python into 'real' code. That is, many of the things that we've learned in Make files won't be applicable to the code that we're going to write. The code will still be Python, so you'll have to know when to use stuff, however, we're going to try to make it more than just a Makefile. Instead, we're going to try to get more useful code out of it. This is the first version of this article. If you notice any mistakes then please let me know.

The first thing we're going to do is create a 'small' project. In this project, we're going to have just two functions, mine, and print. We're going to make these functions run as a single module so that they can be unit tested. We're going to use a library called requests to make our functions more interactive, and useful.

First of all, we're going to import it. We're going to use a library called 'requests' so that we can use it to get data from the web. This is going to be used to get data from the online cryptocurrency exchange, Poloniex. We need to use a library so we can write code that is a lot shorter and easier to read. We're going to use a library called 'requests' to make getting data from the Poloniex API very easy and break down some of the hard parts of doing things.

We're going to ask the Poloniex web API to give us a list of the online wallets. We will be using the 'requests' library again to make life a lot easier as well as bigger. We're also going to need to be able to see how much each one has so that we will use the json() function from the 'requests' module to make this easy to read. We're going to be looking at the amount of money each wallet has, and the Poloniex API is going to give us that.

We will also assume that we have a website that comes from https: We assume that we have a script which deals with 'Hello World' by using 'print.' We also assume that we have a module which deals with 'printing' data. We need a 'print' function that we can use. We also need a function to handle our data. We need something that we can run, display the data, and then get feedback. This is a simple project that is good for testing

Finally, we'll need to write a description for the project. This is just something that we can do to help us when writing our code. We will also need to describe what is our 'output' and 'input' to the project. We will also need to talk about 'safety.' We will also need to prove our 'correctness.' Correctness means that we only work when we have the right input. Correctness helps us to write code that is easier to write and work with. We will also compare our code from today to what a plain text file would look like.

www.ingramcontent.com/pod-product-compliance
Lightning Source LLC
La Vergne TN
LVHW051230050326
832903LV00028B/2324